GW00818516

A TIME

of My

LIFE

A
TIME
of My
LIFE

MO RUDLING

IN THE 1960S, A YOUNG NURSE SETS OFF
ON A BIG ADVENTURE TO THE ATOLLS...

Matador
9 Priory Business Park,
Wistow Road, Kibworth Beauchamp,
Leicestershire. LE8 0RX
Tel: 0116 279 2299
Email: books@troubador.co.uk
Web: www.troubador.co.uk/matador
Twitter: @matadorbooks

ISBN 978 1784624 200

British Library Cataloguing in Publication Data.
A catalogue record for this book is available from the British Library.

Printed and bound by CPI Group (UK) Ltd, Croydon, CR0 4YY
Typeset in 11pt Aldine401 BT by Troubador Publishing Ltd, Leicester, UK

Matador is an imprint of Troubador Publishing Ltd

Prelude

Even today, many people will be unaware of the existence of particular coral islands close to the equator. (Although I myself settled on one, when I was six or seven, I should say though, this was purely imaginative, hooked as I was on one particular story book.)

In the 1960s however, I took off to one in reality, to what was then known as Tarawa, when I was in my twenties.

Certainly previously, during the Second World War, Americans had never heard of the place, so were shocked when they read in newspapers, that 3,000 of their men, U.S. troops, had either died or were wounded, following three days of intensive fighting there. These men had approached on the Pacific Ocean by boat, it was then necessary to wade 500 yards on foot through the shallow lagoon, whilst under fire from the resident Japanese. The Japanese had taken over what *was* a British Colony (although the British, sensing what was happening, had already departed). However, in due course, *they* (the Japanese) were more or less wiped out: 475 men being killed, or else shooting themselves, rather than be captured.

Obviously quite a few years have now passed, and we have entered a new century. (Though with this story, somehow, it doesn't always seem that long ago. I'm still using straw tablemats made and given to me there!) As well, prior to *this* time, I'd already moved around this world quite a bit. Something to do with escapism no doubt, but being a trained nurse and midwife, in those days I was enabled. I'd also much curiosity. (Began with me being a 'Ten-pound pom', though of course that's another story.)

In this case though, a contract was obtained from the British Colonial Service, which, together with travel documents, meant I was committed to undertake two years' service as a nursing-sister, this without holidays, on Tarawa. (Now known as Kiribati, for together with Tuvalu, gained independence in 1978.)

Remote though it remains, many *may* be made aware of it on New Year's Eve, on T.V. It's when girls wearing grass skirts and floral head garlands are seen, welcoming its beginning – for out west it's where the world's rising sun *first* rises.

It's also one of the smallest of 'countries', my area part of five narrow atolls, all no more than five metres above sea level, and all no more than a few miles wide. It currently leaves me worried for with the world facing global warming and seas rising, such places are likely to disappear.

1.

Information about the Gilbert Islands, with a population of around 3,000,000 spread in a chain of 17 coral atolls, was learnt to deal in fishing and farming for copra. I'd then the need to obtain all the requirements in terms of uniform and other tropical clothing, plus crockery and cooking materials, as well as a mosquito net. All these were bought from Harrods, London, for shops on my island were non-existent. That's to say other than a grocery store with provisions obtained from Australia, and these no more frequently than monthly by either boat or plane – for yes, there was an air strip, used if sky or sea proved not too stormy.

The island's own edible supply was mainly just fish and coconuts, although with some paw-paws, some breadfruit – grown in soil that had had to be put there. Water supplies were mainly obtained following rain and collected from steep palm-covered roofs, and electricity wired from a generator.

It was then, Friday 8th March, 1968, that I took off, driven through London to the airport, knowing for a time I was leaving 'this land', creating some nostalgia. It seems as though one's eyes are suddenly opened on such occasions. When the writer H.V. Morton was asked on one occasion where *he* was travelling, he replied, 'To London! It happens to be via the continent.'

My last impressive view of England was Windsor Castle, this day bathed in golden sunlight.

When next I had an impressive viewing, now through my plane window, Ireland was seen below, spread out like a relief map. Following that though, as by now we were high above the Atlantic Ocean, all that could be viewed was cloud. (And no heavenly angels.)

The Boeing 707 flew at around 500 m.p.h. to America – New York was then reached, although having arrived here one's watch required backward timing. So, strange to say, I had arrived before starting! Here too, following disembarkation from the plane, I'd a two-and-a-half-hour wait before taking off again, in this case, eventually, to Fiji (that's to say prior to landing at San Francisco then the island of Honolulu).

The journey had now become trying, this delay leaving me pacing about the airport lounge from which there was no exit.

"If yur servin', why aren't ya attendin' us?" some woman, seated with a group at a table accosted me. She seemed to think I was the waitress, but just not in the mood. And what did I think? – Why is it so many American women are seen to wear silly sequined hairnets, and even sunglasses, inside?

Eventually, aboard again, I had mentally to prepare myself for another American stop, which in due course would be San Francisco. Timewise it was 1.30p.m., although 4p.m., in New York. For myself though, it should have been 10p.m., *and* I had missed my dinner.

Americans could be seen studying their holiday itineraries, the plane now zooming south-westwards, over the Pacific Ocean and to the American island of Honolulu.

When we had this brief landing I had to stretch my legs again, and off the plane, this time, felt the soft, wrap-around warmth of the climate. I was aware of the almost overwhelming smell of no doubt abundant frangipani. (From which, by the by, a 16th century Italian marquis used the perfume for scenting gloves). Of those Americans who, like myself, returned for the next take-off, many now wore delicate pink and cream head garlands, made up from the flowers; the scent here, soon heavy and heavenly.

I'd been travelling now for such a long time that I had begun to feel detached due to tiredness, yet unable to sleep other than briefly. Even though darkness had now descended, with lighting on the plane diminished, I raised my window blind for a brief moment. I was glad I did as I became aware of how many bright shooting stars could be seen, seeming like tears to slide down a cheek.

Having crossed over the International Date Line, the plane began to circle around and wind down, eventually landing at Fiji's Nadi Airport. And here I really did say goodbye to *that* plane. Now, too, I really was aware the climate was tropical. Thus, for survival, I had to strip and change, but with nowhere to do so other than in the loo. It must have been here the mossies attacked me. However, I'd a good immune system in this respect due to many bites received in the past, therefore these bites remained small, not becoming saucer-shaped itches.

Then out into the small waiting room, I found refreshing passion-fruit juice available. The waitress attending, quite uninhibitedly, sang a Fijian song as welcome (I myself the only person now waiting). Male Fijian cleaners however, their job no doubt done, were seen seated now on benches.

They were fast asleep though, eyes closed, but still grasping their broomsticks before them.

At 8a.m. I boarded a thirty-seater de Havilland, about to take off to Tarawa. It had a fortnightly run, although I had hoped it would be delayed, giving me a two-week holiday in Suva. However, it did then take off, although it required a refuelling at Funafuti. And here, it seemed to me, the population of the whole island appeared to watch the procedure.

Arrival at Tarawa was around 4.30p.m.; its hospital matron, Jenny Hopkinson, was there to meet me as I stepped forth from the plane. And my! How the heat now hit me as I stepped forth.

It's practically always around 90°F., with humidity to match; dry for long periods, although rain, when it does descend, is likely to be heavy. But…

"Welcome!" I found myself greeted, before both of us, somewhat formally, then shook hands.

Jenny's a couple of years older than myself, but our height and weight are similar. However, she has almost blonde hair – my own being rather mousy. (And I know there's no hairdresser available, we have to chop our own.)

Jenny, I learnt, attended a well-known London private school before becoming a debutant, where Jenny's father, when in London, signs the *palace* book to say so.

The reason I go into all this is because I myself (consequently) have decided, I'll breathe not a word about my own background – far too rough and tumble I thought. (And well, already I'd learnt, people unknowing thought otherwise.)

4

But, back to the present time, the here and now. Jenny and I *must* have *something* similar within us, both having decided to train as nurses. It's a vocational job that means earning little money and achieving but lowly status. Training too, more or less, meant largely dealing with bedpans and bandages.

And now – the present time. Well we've both decided to work somewhere as cut off as Tarawa – a bit like both of us deciding we'll both be nuns.

For some reason too, a film I'd seen came into my head although *of course* not at all related, in which Humphrey Bogart, acting as a rough character owning a boat, and Kathleen Hepburn, a nun, set off together, in a wartime escape over east African river rapids, in order to blow up a German boat. It's docked on the lake they eventually hoped to reach.

Did I really think my own future work would turn out to be as tough? Ridiculous!

Soon I was whizzed away on the back of Jenny's scooter whilst clinging to her back as we sped along a sandy road, leading to what was to be my lodging. This was found to be a one-storey building, with wooden floors inside, and windows, although without glass, meshed against mosquitoes. Its steep pitched roof has been covered with palm leaves, collected perhaps after storms when trees become tempest-razed and broken.

I found that just a few steps were required in order to reach what was a soft sandy beach, giving way to the turquoise-coloured tidal lagoon. (Woe to so many U.S. troops during the war.) The lagoon is edged by an erupting coral reef that then gives way to deep ocean – the royal-blue-coloured Pacific. A constant roar is heard from waves that beat against this reef, through which – just a small gap – boat owners must cleverly negotiate.

Actually, already known to me, a few British, on arrival here by plane, have immediately become scared when they hear that roar and see those waves! They think the sea might anytime engulf all land and people, so straightaway must reboard the plane they came on – too afraid to remain.

I myself have remained so in due course found myself taken inside my future lodging, here found to have a desk, table, and cane chairs in its living room, two bedrooms, a kitchen with a stove *and* refrigerator, as well as a shower room.

I have temporary use of transit-box items, namely sheets, towels, and crockery, things I can use until, by sea, my own trunk of luggage arrives. As well – how thoughtful of Jenny. On my desk I found a stamped aerogramme enabling immediate send-off of a postal communication, this to those back home, who must know of one's arrival. Post goes out on the plane I came in on, a service which after today is not available for another fortnight.

N.B. *The writing that continues, remains based on the diary I kept at the time. I have however made some current additions. Please forgive me though, if some thoughts have, over time become distorted.*

11*th* *March '68*
Having woken early I felt a need to to look around my area.

On the ocean side of this land-strip, the wind was found to blow, waving especially the coconut trees. A boy wearing just a lavalava was seen climbing one, easy, for steps have been chopped into its trunk. He then collected sap from it, singing – this I've learnt to ward off evil spirits during the process. What's obtained is for toddy. Whether it will be fermented and made alcoholic – I can't say.

Three or four dolphins were also briefly seen, leaping from the deep blue sea here. One feels one should also hear them shout for joy. Seeing them seemed to have the same effect on myself!

Walking back to my place, smoke was seen rising from open fires in the leprosarium, they were cooking breakfast fish. They live in traditional raised places made from coconut wood, and with blinds to pull down for shelter and privacy. Soon, seeing me, they broke out into harmonised song. No inhibition whatsoever.

This morning the Medical Superintendant's wife who introduced herself as Mrs Marshall (my, names *are* formal – at least at present) collected me to take to the store so I could shop. A fair selection of groceries were found to be available, although expensive – unsurprising, for they've to be flown a long way. Did someone say Australia?

Later I had coffee with her at her place, and saw she had a marvellous collection of seashells.

Back at my place, I found a girl, Mimoa, waiting there for me. She told me she is sixteen years old and reminds me of a painting by Gauguin.

She also said she speaks some English and desires to be my house girl. I tell her to come back tomorrow.

Come evening I was again collected, in order to be taken and formally introduced to the Resident Commissioner.

A few of us had bundled ourselves into a Land Rover driven by Joe (here to produce a thesis about how rats may be controlled) and were soon zooming along our sandy road.

But what a dusty run – even with windows fully open. I'd been told to be formal, so had obeyed: white cotton gloves accompanying my frock. What can I say? Not only did it prove difficult not to sweat profusely, but also difficult to keep clean.

Nevertheless we reached our formal destiny, and following introductions were offered alcoholic cocktails, plus some light tasty eatables (noted to be on G.R. plates!). Dozens of guests, aside from ourselves – teaching, doing V.S.O. work etc. – were then expected to circulate around.

Those drinks were offered, and received, continuously, until 'God Save the Queen' was played by a uniformed Gilbertese band to indicate 'finato'. Their instruments were maybe affected by humidity, as they sounded a bit off-key.

That evening, I'd another invite back at Doctor and Mrs Marshall's place. I like them a lot. Doctor, I've now learnt, nearly died from septicaemia not so long ago, following a cut from live coral. Apart from coral's exquisite designs, it can be covered in bacteria.

In due course a delectable supper was produced; a little worrying for I know in due course, I will be expected to offer my own dinner party.

12th March '68
Jenny showed me around what was found to be a spread-out hospital made up of people with diverse complaints.

First visit was to the leprosarium, with, I'd say, around twenty people suffering from chronic leprosy.

Neither Jenny or myself have previously come across

leprosy, although I have heard about it. It's mentioned, I believe, biblically. During that time sufferers went around ringing a bell, whilst at the same time declaring, 'Unclean! Unclean!'

Great progress has though been made though since 1944, with the introduction of Dapsone (and we *do* have some here) together with being able to successfully combat its causative organism by being given BCG vaccination as prophylaxis. (Against TB also, so I am myself protected.)

Here too patients keep a few pigs in a pen, and chickens wander about. They have been donated (by New Zealand) a canoe in which to set out to sea and fish, fish being the predominant part of their diet.

A male dresser – Putuki, wearing a lavalava with a red-cross printed on it, hands out daily drugs.

Inmates all appear to be happy.

Putuki also attends to patients – around the same number, in the mental hospital – or asylum which Gilbertese prefer to still call it. They believe, as the British used to, that some people may mentally be adversely affected by the *luna* (moon) causing intermittent insanity. Well here they *do* get drug treatment for the madness – often Largactil, but E.C.T. is sometimes medically used to combat it. (Otherwise, so I was told, such a patient *not* admitted to the hospital, may be tied to a tree untill they are exhausted enough to be undone.)

Most people here have a long-term condition, this is therefore their home.

Inside it's rather grim and needs cleaning and painting badly. One man has murdered – voices told him to do it, whilst a young woman, wishing to escape this world tried to do so walking into the ocean – although, obviously, she was rescued.

Still on tour I met Howard. He's Australian, although here he intends to remain. He has in fact recently married a Gilbertese girl.

Howard, being the chief pharmacist, showed me around his dispensary. Again though, I have to say, it was a bit grubby, although, of course, sand *does* blow about. Beer bottles are in great demand for dispensed medicines. (But who in the first place drinks it all? Beer, I mean.)

Within the bulk store there was discovered to be a rather rusty X-ray machine. It, like many things, has been carted back from that isolated place akin to Christmas Island (isolated following the long past H-bomb tests) together with an outboard motor for a boat.

I was told though, we have no Ergometrine, given (at least back home) to women who have just given birth in order to minimise bleeding from the uterus. Perhaps I have to get used to the situation *here*. Medical supplies are limited – getting stuff here, yes, but also a *very* limited amount of British money can be spent.

The rest of the hospital was found to consist of a small private ward for the occasional Brit taken ill, obstetric ward (with limitations as mentioned), male, female and children's wards, together with an isolation unit for those suffering from TB. PAS for this disease cannot be used here, for I'm told it would deteriorate in this climate.

A few cases of infant malnutrition occur; their appearance the sad reality of those OXFAM adverts seen.

Trainee nurses have trestle tables with benches set up in their dining room. Whilst training and resident here, the diet supplied by the hospital often consists of tinned corned beef, together with locally grown breadfruit, pumpkin, and babai. At teatime they'll have bread and jam.

Nearly forgot to mention, the afternoon excursion I had with Jenny in order to purchase that breadfruit. We travelled to the village of Bonriki in a V.W. van donated by UNICEF. Our hospital secretary equipped with money box, accompanied us.

Beneath the shade of a tree, fruit had been laid out by locals on a mat for inspection, they were all hopeful of a purchase.

The fruit is green, lobular, and seedless (never seen one before), each the size of a large potato. When roasted it becomes like new bread, but if then dried, will keep for ages.

A family group of mothers and children stood around, looking rather poor, so no doubt anxious to receive a sale.

I thought much of the fruit, looking scabby was diseased, and when I expressed some concern, a mature woman nodded, which in Gilbertese meant 'No'. Anyway, with just two crops yearly, the fruit is needed badly for food. Here too I *should* add, when back at the hospital, *our own* Gilbertese said it wasn't diseased at all.

13ᵗʰ March '68
I had ward rounds early this morning with M.S., acute patients' treatment together with their progress needing to be assessed. My own job in this respect, will be mainly supervisory for the hospital now has its own trained people, running the wards and dealing with surgery etc.

Hoped I looked just as smart as he did. He, *almost* old enough to be 'dad', seen to be wearing pressed white shorts

11

like a continental sea-captain. And actually, 'water-wise', when I asked him if it was alright to swim in the lagoon, said "O.K. That's if you're not agin the likes of warm pea-soup".

My evening always seems to be spent having a meet-up with others. So, finding myself invited to Jenny's place, met a particular friend of hers, Judy, sociologist, together with two young blokes, V.S.O.s dealing with agriculture (?? what can *ever* be additional to what now grows here, mainly palm-trees) and the manager of the very tiny 'hotel'. (A guest most likely to be some M.P. from the U.K., undertaking monetory investigations.)

In Jenny's garden we all sipped beer beneath *her* palm-trees, where it came into my mind, a bit of Philip Larkin:

'The moon is full tonight
And hurts the eyes,
It is so definite and bright.

Later, as always, a lovely meal was provided. Food is bought from our grocery with its imported stuff, for we mustn't devastate locals of their own fish and coconuts. Tasted good and didn't hurt the tongue.

14ᵗʰ March '68

Today's round with M.S. had to do with looking around the leprosarium. Patients can be especially prone to hurt themselves, because limbs often have lack of feeling. With many too, disfiguring nodules can be seen on ears, and face.

Eventually we all met up in their maneaba, or speak house. (Donated by N.Z. Leper Trust). Space-wise it was found to be large, like a village hall, its steep pitched thatch extending down to deep eaves, leaving it cool.

M.S. greeted all – "Konamauri…" asking then their chief if they had any requests or complaints.

"We want some rice" he responded, "And some paint for the boat."

They also wished to go on a picnic all together, but learnt this wasn't possible. They are however allowed to visit an outside relative. Though I suppose they have been told to avoid touching.

Following this visit then we walked to see the mental patients (or lunatics as I've said Gilbertese wish them to be labelled). One old man was found to wear nothing but a sack. Several year's supply of lavalavas had created a stack of neat parcels in his cell, these though were apparently not to his taste.

Today ended with an evening session at Joe's house, nothing to do with a lecture regarding the habits of rats, but several of us instead endeavouring to learn to speak Gilbertese. There's actually a printed book to help us, within which the first comment noticed concerned the mosquito:

"Moan te kamimi wina" meaning, 'very wonderful is its mouth' – surely a rather debatable point.

15ᵗʰ March '68

Today our Chief Medical Officer (admin.) whisked me away for a personal introduction to His Honour, Resident Commissioner Mr V.J. Andersen (C.M.G., O.B.E., V.R.D.). He is from New Zealand originally, so it's no wonder he was found to be so much easier (I imagine) to talk to than a Brit.,given this formal position.

Later we went on to the treasury enabling me to cash

my traveller's cheques. The Australian dollar is the money used, albeit there's nothing to buy other than food and drink. Dissapointed therefore not to receive gold ingots in exchange.

On return, time enough to get around the hospital. Everything satisfactory.

As is so often the case, was again asked to join several at a buffet supper, this time given by Elizabeth. (Who, as mentioned, is herself from New Zealand, and now prepares a report for W.H.O.) Methinks, again – can one receive better to eat at London's Savoy?

I still keep bumping into new people, doing this and that. This time a young man employed by OXFAM – Coconut-Officer(??)

16th March '68

The hospital event of the day has involved the 'tidy round'. Young men even climbed into the rafters to dust. When I myself inspected I could see that something had been done, nevertheless, could be somewhat improved. Outside the TB ward I was meant to be impressed, for here a floral arrangement made of paper and on sticks had been pushed into the ground. Actually, sometimes a nurse will turn up on duty wearing a floral decoration instead of her cap. It's her own particular outlook.

17th March '68 (Sunday)

Last night, as usual, remained hot and humid. Hoping to sleep I was therefore naked and atop the bed sheets. Did drop off, but not for long, for I found myself, not exactly being eaten alive, *but*, having hundreds of ants crawling all over me, even attemping to make it up my nostrils, and inside my ears.

I don't so much mind occasionally eating a few, when they've become cooked in bread (even though I believed at first, our cook kneaded *currant* bread) but I definitely dislike sharing bed and body with them.

Gave myself an emergency shower, after which I was cleansed.

At 7.30p.m. I attended the church service given by the London Missionary Society with Jenny. The small round church is simple and beautiful with a predominant cross inside made from a split coconut trunk.

We sang 'Praise to the Lord...' with belief, Jenny accompanying our singing with her flute.

18th March '68

Today I have been initiated into the 'rude elements' of what might be termed 'bush nursing'.

Naliere, a young man found to be suffering from cirrhosis of the liver, last night had a sudden, severe haematemesis. It couldn't be compensated. So he died.

Tongoa also died this morning, after colonic lavage – he had a dissecting aneurysm.

Then this evening, a young woman who had been admitted to the hospital who was found to have placenta previa with her pregnancy, developed early labour, so began heavy bleeding. As you might have guessed, here we have no stored blood not even plasma, and although our Gilbertese doctor went to search for his donor – indeed, found her – he came back to find it was too late. Our patient had just passed away.

Of note, too, is the fact that nurses here become very afraid when cases like this arise – indeed I found most who previously dealt with care, now had to run away! – Methinks anyway, this woman should have had an early caesarian.

Another thought. Perhaps all or our nurses might like to have their own blood typed, someone able to then quickly donate when the need arises. Such a suggestion, really not meant as hubris. Anyway, I'll speak to the Red Cross woman about possible *expatriate* volunteer donors.

19th March '68

Twins born today! I'd palpated the woman who had only just arrived, but didn't diagnose *the two*. Neither did our local doctor!

Twin one, breech, was 4lb 2oz – twin two, only 2lb 9oz. I hope we can get them to thrive. The smallest nearly didn't make it at birth – however, we will do our best.

20th March '68

Just abed last night when I heard clap-clapping across my wooden floor. Sounded, it seemed, like a toddler daughter, aiming to walk wearing mummy's high-heels. What I saw though at first spooked me, as seen to be a huge, huge live crab. Don't think he harms, can't climb a bed leg, but perhaps he'll eat the ants.

At the hospital come morning, felt our twins were thriving. We have no incubators, but in this climate – high temperature and humidity, this may for such infants be beneficial.

As usual – perhaps because I'm newish (only been here ten days!) another dinner invite, this from M.S. and wife, with other guests: CMO and a Judge trainee.

21st March '68
I feel I'm finding my feet in the hospital now, although I *should* be absorbing more Gilbertese names.

Later had my evening dinner with Miss Blake, our sister tutor. Just the two of us, she told me I could now call her Enid. She's a sweet person, and, as I believe I've said, comes over as genteel. She also seems to me somewhat frail. Before we began our meal, she called in her cat wailing, 'Tab…by…' her voice most definitely quavery.

22nd March '68
Much of my time today was spent trying to organise the obstetric ward. The best policy is now, I feel, to work on a particular ward, rather than flit all over and achieve very little. I was surprised to find that not all babies end up being entirely breast-fed. But what a sad situation! I discovered that our colony nurse here made up an infant feed by putting in forty teaspoons of sugar to the pint! Of course babe loves it. But…!

23rd March '68
The smallest twin died in the night. Suffered, I think, from an internal haemorrhage.

On the ward this morning I found the oxygen cylinder

would not administer. The machine that carries it is linked to one of nitrogen. As the switches had been altered (I did ask doctor not to) this, if used as an attempt to resuscitate, would have been what was administered, so…

I remained here for a large part of the day, here being where one might weep. Found too many rusty instruments, together with finger-cots perished, plus oh dear, dear, dear – dirt, dirt, dirt. Or do I mean inevitable dust, dust, dust.

Suppose we Brits endeavour to bring about a different culture. And the training here, concerning this, is relatively short-lived. What I say too can be misunderstood, and that which I regard as *constructive* criticism re. this or that, only induces a frightened silence.

On another topic (escape from upsets), I've barely mentioned this island. I've not yet fully explored, as have no transport. But, when Elizabeth (WHO) leaves, she says I can have her bike.

From this house of mine though, as I've indicated, I look out toward the ocean. The reef is about one hundred yards from shore and when it's high tide, the sea beyond, edged rough and spumous with surf, soon becomes several hundred feet deep.

Ashore though, coconuts grow everywhere (except of course on that air-strip) their green-brown frond-like palms, constantly moving and rustling in the breeze, trunks slender with a graceful curve.

That toddy in fact, is collected twice a day, whilst copra, only export I'd guess, is seen drying, a few piles spread out around on the ground.

As for Gilbertese women, all wear a wrap of colourfully printed cotton – material from Fiji, whilst men just the lavalava, *their* top often kept bare (mmm…). But our doctors,

18

aiming to look professional, they wear khaki shorts with white cotton tops.

For special occasions a particular skirt can be worn by both male and female, made up of grassy material, woven from the long narrow leaves of the pandanus.

Some of these shrubs grow four foot high, and having twisted stems and aerial roots, it's why it's sometimes called screw-pine.

Because the soil here is more or less non-existent, it is difficult to grow flowers or vegetables. One does though see some scarlet hibiscus, and equally colourful bougainvillea. There's even a little grass in places.

It's O.K. though to travel the road, either by bike, or car (not many of the latter, thank goodness) although there is no bitumen, so does create much dust, *a great cloud* of this whenever a plane lands. But that vivid turquoise lagoon – I know I repeat myself, this offers clear vision from its fine golden beach, shaded of course by the coconuts.

And we Brits – *we've* made our mark on this colony. For ourselves and in Bikenibeu, have all amenities required. Islanders themselves though must use nakataris, whenever a certain need arises. These are privies, seen here and there, several feet out in the lagoon. They are approached from the beach, by means of a raised tree trunk. A good balancing act is required, for it seems to me, *almost* like the tight-rope used by acrobats. I must admit though, the locals all arrive at their destination without difficulty, a pair of legs frequently seen dangling from the small tin hut devoid of floor. Perhaps I should donate my large trunk – *when* it arrives. It could have one side removed and be upended.

As pointed out, Bikenibeu inhabitants are mostly Government employees, and we in our bungs, we (lucky devils) all have loos etc. Here too, aside from the store, there's a post office, police station and 'hotel', the generating station, plus agricultural and medical departments. In addition there's the K.G.V. (King George) school. The surroundings though remain very attractive – just like one imagines a desert island to be, although not in the manner sometimes portrayed, uninhabited and desolate.

The climate as mentioned is always hot and humid, although it does have a constant breeze. I'm surprised though to see only a few birds, even though a particular poem did come into my head:

It's a warm wind, the west wind, full of birds' cries,

And I never hear the bird's cries but tears are in my eyes…

This though refers to back home.

There are however many cats, good in a sense I guess, because, so I'm told (though haven't seen 'em), many rats. There are dogs too – all mongrels, but not *so* many, and some people keep a few pigs and chickens. There are no other animals (aside from humans) no snakes, only scorpions and centipedes that can sting.

***

As for myself. Well I do feel cut off from the outside world, can only get the Australian News on my radio at 7a.m., and this gives out little world news. Neither have I seen a newspaper since I've been here. As for books; well I'm told not to expect that trunk of mine for six months – or more, it coming on a ship, or rather ships, not a plane.

In general, as I've recognised, life here gets lived Colonial style. Plus, seen in the hospital, times when things go wrong, enough to lead to stress, at the same time, sadden and frustrate. But, in spite of the drawbacks mentioned, plus those weevils in the flour, few fresh vegetables, bad eggs, and ants that tried to eat me, I feel I must plod on. No I don't mean it to sound so dogged. The wider vision is that I see both place and people as lovely.

Tonight was a special occasion, as I found myself invited to a performance of Tabiteuean dancing at the K.G.V. school.

There were several dancers, men, women and small girls. Males wore woven mats over their lavalavas, tied for hold-on by a long sash, whilst females, low on the hips, black grass skirts. All had a wreath of flowers like rose-mallow hibiscus around head and neck, flowers also attached as bracelets and armlets.

They formed a line before their audience, this formation then moving backwards and forwards, as they clapped their own hands hard together, before against those of each other. Then, remaining stationary, they began stamping, females also wiggling hips to give the impression of a boat rocking on water. Men's facial expression had also markedly altered – reminding me of those NZ ruggers, before commencement of their game, fearful with tongues sticking out. Women as a contrast looked serene with gentle smiles.

To sum-up, the dance, vibrant and exciting, was performed with gusto, as well – forgot to mention – accompanied here and there by some uninhibited, harmonious singing. Strange though, the language used with the singing, had, as was later explained, been handed down for generations, it not fully understood by themselves. Perhaps because this 'Old Gilbertese' expressed, as with us, old Anglo-Saxon.

21

After the performance the school's headmaster suggested the dancers receive a drink plus a wrapped gift presentation.

"Is that alright?" he asked the boys at the school, though "Yes Sir", was a subdued response.

"It's *not* alright, I can tell," he then said. "How would you do it?"

"Well Sir, we would like to give them a good sprinkling of talc powder…"

"Very well.I'll leave it to you," he says.

24th March '68 (Sunday)
Today I've had a work day-off, with Jenny on hospital call for emergencies.

I know I've hardly mentioned Jenny. I guess in general, we both undertake our separate nine-to-five roles. J. buys and deals with all hospital food, and deals with money spent on acquirements in general – bit of a headache. We both though, on the whole, meet for a coffee mid-morning, I then have a welcome Darjeeling-tea with her in her shady garden, come the end of the day.

As to today however, the Crawfords (married couple – Scottish docs, often out and about performing preventative minor surgery) hired our hospital motorboat having arranged to take a small group of us as far as Bonriki for a picnic.

On arrival we all swam in what was here crystal clear water.

"Can I borrow your snorkel?" I asked Crawford, to find then, what I never would have known about – so many little coloured fish, darting between vivid fronds of seaweed, together with an equally illuminated view of coloured shells

22

and coral. Not so far beyond, was the white wall of foam at the passage where the ocean breaks over reef. Here it really could be heard to roar, this too was somehow exhilarating.

Eventually we'd all tired ourselves enough in the water to then sit on the beach, beneath the shade of palms. The palms here seemed as though they were 'new', for leaves shone and shimmered in the sun with a wetness (like babes at their birth). Further inland it would have been impossible to sit for vegetation here was so dense. But where *we* were, we'd spread our mat on the golden sand, as though we were the Famous Five, here to have our picnic and drink some beer.

Returning home, all were tired and sunburned, yet we said mentally refreshed.

25th March '68
On return from work today, I was practically poisoned by Mimoa.

I had left a note for her to get turps. at the store. It's sold in squash bottles, and is colourless. I keep squash bottles of water in the fridge for drinking, and happened to notice *four* bottles there instead of three. Sniffed all four and rectified the mistake.

I wonder if the islanders' drinks in general consist of that toddy… M.S. explained about collection:

Young men always sing, although it's not just because they are happy. They've a purpose – needing to scare away bad influences so that they don't fall from out of the tree. Then:

1. The flower is cut at its end, so that sap drips into their container.
2. This may later be boiled (pity really as the vit.C is destroyed). If however left for some hours, it becomes sour but alcoholic.
3. Each flower, by the way, is shaved down at its end, enabling it to grow again.

27th March '68

No diary entry yesterday. Stuck-in at work, and work at the moment – well it's been to do with repeating myself. As well, at the end of the day, I found myself too tired.

Today though I'll record having had dinner with the Crawfords.

Worms! Must have been those beach ones. Nice flavour, but rather tough.

29th March '68

Early a.m. out on the boat again, this time to Betio via the ocean, a matter of work business. I found myself accompanied by our local, well-established Gilbertese doctor. He undertakes any necessary surgery, a well-trained Fijian nurse assisting. Both of us found we must sit atop the canvas rooftop, rather than be suffocated by petrol fumes below.

The journey took around an hour. The weather, as usual, was hot, but not enough to suspend conversation; this is when Dr. Flood (? surname) related his amazing personal story.

It was an event that had occurred some years ago. He and a friend, again on the small craft, had gone fishing, on this very same stretch of water. They were, however, caught in a storm, which left them drifting miles and miles, (or did he say many knots) both north and westward.

Soon they ran out of fuel. It was hopeless to even consider an attempt to swim ashore, as they counted *thirteen* sharks in the water around them.

Thus they remained at sea for thirteen days. At first they ate raw fish, but later decided not to eat at all because it increased their thirst, and by now they were reduced to drinking their urine. But then they found themselves able to collect a little rain water.

Eventually they were picked up by Japanese fishermen near the Carolines – fortunate as we're not now at war with them – then gave them the boat as a gesture of gratitude. And this is a debt he *still* owes the government.

On arrival at Betio it was my job to visit the dispensary. I found it to be primitive. The small wooden building had a queue that extended outside, way beyond the entrance, with all patients more or less requiring treatment for bad leg scratches. When it was their turn, still standing, the bad leg was raised to rest upon a blood-soiled foot bar. And here, the nurse with forceps holding a swab, dipped it into gentian violet, then dabbed. Thing is, the same pair of forceps was used over and over on everyone – not even cleansed – so that as far as germs were concerned, they might spread person to person, rather than be attacked.

Hope my explanation to nurse will now have rectified the matter.

Later, had a revolting lunch-meal at what passed as a Chinese restaurant. Little more than a pile of sticky rice.

As to Betio. Here it felt especially hot, that breeze, for some reason, diminished. Nevertheless, before getting back on the boat, felt I should stagger along to see the war-memorial.

This had been erected to honour those British people, who, prior to the Japanese invasion did not leave their posts – did not depart by canoe, so as a consequence, ended up murdered.

On the beach here too were a couple of amphibious tanks of American origin. The U.S. attack, although eventually successful, was timed badly so that their arrival at low tide, created a bloody massacre. Moments now of thoughts about such an issue, always leaves one feeling sad.

But back at Bikenibeu I found myself back to the here and now. So much nicer here too than Betio, I might add.

I'd left a note for Mimoa to collect some flowers for me, and on arrival home, found I'd acquired a whole bucket full.

"Where from?" I asked the girl, amazed. She though refused to respond, just giggled then ran away.

The flowers were needed for the 'Box-Party' here. A number of us females had made a decorated box having the equivalence of a picnic basket, this with a meal for two packed inside. Later raffled, the money collected was for the Red Cross.

31st March '68 (Another Sunday)
Out in the lagoon again; this time to the tiny island of Bikeman.

It was low tide though, so to get aboard the boat meant we all had to wade waist-deep for yards and yards through the water – *and* whilst treading on more squidgy bêche-de-mer.

I don't know how, but I managed to eventually climb aboard, *but* without my chicken pie, which I'd held aloft with difficulty, but getting wet, was ruined.

Doing twelve knots, it was a journey of just over an hour. The tiny uninhabited island we arrived at, was found to have another marvellous little beach – bleached by exposure to sunlight, and, as with all such places, having its centre made up of trees and scrubs giving shade.

Peter (M.S.) and his wife Jean later arrived to join us, they having used their Gilbertese canoe. Such a Pacific dugout, made from a single pine tree, is fitted with an outrigger – and like some yachts, skims pretty fast across the water, one sitting on it, rather than in it.

1ˢᵗ April '68
There are times when abed, not exactly tucked up, but there, when I'll receive a request to see someone in the hospital. It is usually a pregnant woman whose labour has progressed, the note often, as last night, touchingly quaint:

> *'Dear——, Here we have a new antenatal named Teuatake*
> *from labour line she have a first baby please would*
> *see her. Show been discharge last night P/R 4"*
> *fingers light away palpation was engaged.*
> *She is on first stage. Yours sincerely, Emire.'*

Come morning on my tour, I've to read hospital ward reports from the night nurses. So here's one of those:

All found comfortable on bed most of time during night.
All their temperature have taken and no one raised his
temperature from them. No one complain the whole night.'

3rd April '68

Had another p.m. invite to the Residency – today for dinner.

As usual though, all attenders get greeted by H.H. (And I *don't* mean His Highness, it's mere reference to our High Commissioner. (Our reference – are we mistaken??)

All who've been invited, as before, then stand, cruise, and try to be sociable, helped by the drinks received. Our efficient waiters once again are seen to wear their pressed lavalavas, this with a red stripe down one side.

Eventually, when the soup arrived one could sit down. My napkin was blown by a breeze though, part of it then in my soup. No-one noticed however, and being the size of either a small tablecloth, or else a very large napkin, I could fold it in half to use.

After our meal, it was the duty of all to be up once again to mingle and talk, this as our coffee was taken. On this occasion I met up with H.H. and his wife, and had what passed as a chat.

"And what do you think of Tarawa?" he asked, and myself, being not fully aware of its smallness – having still not seen the whole of the island, said,

"It gives me a sense of freedom, gazing out at the blue ocean. Even though I've no boat, and of course can't swim away. I know it's quite different, but I'm reminded of the vast, but brown horizons in Australia."

Mrs Hamblet then said she feels the opposite, "shut in" as she put it, "on this tiny isolated plot. You see, I miss so much the hills and rivers." Now though, H.H. suggested she climbed a coconut tree – second best to a hill. For, well, as everyone knows, Tarawa is no more than 4ft above sea-level – not anywhere. How fortunate it is that tidal waves are unknown.

7th April '68

It seems to be the season for babies. They've been popping out all over, and with no probs.

Piglets have also been born; a litter of six. I know little about the post-natal care of pigs, but suggested our sow was given milk to drink.

10th April '68

Our hospital cook asked me to look in at the kitchen. He wished me to inspect the flour. This was found to appear not entirely white – much half black. Seemed too to have movement – as though shallow breathing... Oh dear! – Weevils!

My opinion was that it should be dumped – until I inspected stock. *All* bags were found to have holes, for, those creatures within, fulfilled, now wished to get out into the free world.

Myself – facing now the potential problem of literally starving people, suggested cook try using a fine seive before making bread. I will then try a crust myself, and hopefully – hopefully! find it reasonably edible. (A problem Captain Cook once faced at sea.)

Talk about worries concerning certain living creatures. When entering the first ward today, I found a food-thieving cat was being chased by a formidable gang of youths. These young men all *looked* pretty, wearing as they did their floral garlands, but, armed with sticks whilst loudly screeching, "Ah!… Ah!… Ah!…" I soon witnessed what was very brutal assasination of the creature. These were people who showed no respect for the poor animal.

Had not, until today, tasted coconut water. Jenny though soon found a boy who climbed a tree, knocking down then a couple of nuts. (We two of couse, standing well clear.) Then, having descended, with his sharpened stick, split off their husks,this before chopping away one end. I then found myself offered that within, and drinking from the nut, found the clear sweet liquid very refreshing.

P.S. *Have* heard – as a sterile means of hydration, it can be given intravenously.

18th April '68
This weekend found myself busy painting ward lockers. Perhaps we can get the Boy Scouts to finish off.

19th April '68
"Don't you think we might set-up a Central Sterile Supply system, this with dressing packs, in already autoclaved bags?"

My suggestion was put to Matron. After all, these would create: better sterility, better technique, as well as a system more convenient.

Jenny though has a real headache concerning everything obtained. For, as I have mentioned before, there is very little money to be dealt with, coupled with difficulty even obtaining such supplies. My idea therefore gets overruled.

"Nurses anyway", she says, "should be well aquainted with the system of boiling for sterilisation, then laying trays and trolleys. As well, many who we train, will in due course be working on an outer, even more remote island where regular supplies of anything is difficult."

On another topic, our pigs are doing well. It's especially good that we had a litter of seven, because litters here have been smaller – no more than just three or four. As well, if a pig is not fed adequately, self ingestion of foetal pigs occurs.

1st May '68
Re. this diary. Of late I've not felt able to follow close upon my last entry, i.e. the next day. As before, I *am* busy work hours, with some shared on-call night periods, and also, late evening there are the nurses' dormitories to check – to make sure no-one has been abducted. But then – free time – well the tennis court now gets used in spite of climactic heat – *and* I've brought with me a racket, then Monday there's art class, Thursday Gilbertese, and come Sunday, attendance at a church service. Evening dinner invites also continue, so usually I fight against time to get written letters on that mail plane, let alone deal with this diary.

2nd May '68
This evening attended a very relaxed dinner party put on by Howard our pharmacist (from Oz, although here he now

intends to stay) and his Ellice-island wife, found to be an exceptional cook.

To begin, we had fish soup, prepared with raw fish, not cooked but soaked for a time in coconut cream. This latter was made using a mature nut that was grated, then squeezed through muslin to obtain all its moisture. High calorific value, but…

What followed was a mixture of European, Chinese, and Ellice food, all on the same plate, as well composed of a vast quantity: fish, chicken, fried breadfruit, roast potatoes, noodles in sauce, plus vegetables. It will require a day or two to digest and recover from it all.

3rd May '68

Matron – of course Jenny, and I, undertook to observe the practical aspect of the student nurses' examination. I'm afraid it proved something of a fiasco.

Two candidates were asked to lift a patient out of bed – another student acting as such, she though appearing to be twice their weight put together. The technique should have been better – but wasn't, all three of them therefore tumbling to the floor. To be honest it appeared like a comedy show, and when the students *all* burst into laughter, I'd difficulty not doing so myself.

Another observation today, was seeing our Gilbertese surgeon and Fijian theatre sister, undertake a surgical operation.

To begin, a dresser – trained male-nurse, gave what's usual, this being a spinal anaesthetic. Meantime our surgeon, having scrubbed-up, having gowned, then goes to put on sterile rubber gloves. Only the second pair however, did not disintegrate when pulled on, the first pair having obviously rotted as soon in shreds.

Maybe I should not now be criticising, I'm not myself very experienced in the theatre – indeed not as experienced as *these* people, today now observed. Surgery here though, is not highly practised, neither has been medically established for years. As well, today's surgical procedure, did *end-up* cut-and-dried, so shouldn't be called a fiasco. It's just that all instruments used were from a pile, it necessary for the surgeon's attendant to delve. Sometimes too, what she came up with, was not, to begin, what she'd guessed he required.

It left me making a comparison with a theatre sister back home. Although, to begin, her instruments were viewed not held, they might be compared with fanned out playing-cards. Very soon therefore, one got very rapidly pounced upon.

P.S. This record I now type, of thoughts and events experienced way-back, did not for some reason, always get dated.

Bairiki versus Bikenibeu. Darts versus ping-pong. Both games are liked by locals.

Speaking to Johnnie – Kuru's brother, was when these games got discussed, although other 'swings or roundabout' topics, were soon found on the agenda.

What I really mean is, my own opinions were sought regarding this or that, and too on a number of topics. *However*, what initially I hadn't known, but then came to learn – he himself is a member of the House of Representatives. My interrogation thus had to do with what he now wished to put forward in the House, especially theories for the Medical Department.

Aware then of this matter I was horrified and explained, these could only involve the Chief Medical Officer – not myself! – I blush now, I really do, at how thoughtless I can be, at the thought of my own name and suggestions, being brought up at Legislative Assembly.

Jonnie, an Ellice islander was once a Roman-Catholic priest. During his training he was sent to Rome, there receiving in depth, all matters concerning the faith, before his ordination.

Back to his island, soon he married (how could he not), although sad to say, from the church he had to abdicate.

2.

Late May '68
Jenny will be spending some days away, on a tour of the southern Gilberts. So, for the moment, I'm to take over what's usually her job.

A primary task has to do with preparing the hospital menu, which although not very varied, still seems somewhat complex. Foods mostly eaten will be rice, bread, breadfruit, pumpkin, tinned corned beef and fish, although some freshly-caught fish, together with hen's eggs may be purchased from a villager. As a treat, sugar, milk powder, cocoa and coffee, unpacked from boxes initially for troops, but collected from that island now deserted this where they once checked their H bombs, may also be used. Another treat too, will be an occasional pig. Oh too – believe I've previously mentioned, our nurses also have bread, marg. and jam for breakfast.

Complication however arises in dishing out amounts, for our TB patients get served more protein (i.e. tinned meat or fish) whilst patients requiring salt-free diets have first preference of fresh eggs and fish. Lepers too, who live in their grass houses, but have a canoe to fish for themselves, are given extra rice. Each ration, must therefore be calculated, so many ounces per person accordingly.

As before I went off to Bonriki to buy breadfruit, together with some eggs. These were put in a bowl of water first, making sure they didn't float, which happens if they're too old and rotten.

Suppose too, I should mention the need to buy meat and potatoes for the few Europeans admitted to our hospital, for they receive Private treatment.

And by-the-way, I soon found the need to hand over some hospital milk powder contaminated with weevils, this to a *private* pig owner. In return – here's hoping, in time we receive a return.

Early June '68

Jenny's tour, she related, proved exciting. Of the *tiny* islands visited and now medically looked after by dressers, some had not been seen for years. One she met had not even been paid, not since last December. As well, all he had for supplies, was one vial of penicillin, and one Codeine tablet. It proved difficult for him to know how much to order, aside from basic communication. If there is someone who is very sick he endeavours to get him/her on a ship to Tarawa. Mostly though the wait is lengthy, meaning the patient probably ends up dying.

J. had another tale to tell, this one amusing.

"A couple of canoes came out to meet *our* ship, to receive mail and treasury money. Unfortunately though, they became entangled in the rope thrown down to keep them alongside, so capsized. The men though swum around, not only righted their boats, but also collected wet goods.

Next day then, at the post office hut, all mail and paper money was seen bestrewn, pegged on a line to dry."

***

Must say I'm astounded by the bill received from the wholesale society, in connection with food I've bought these past two months. It's over one hundred dollars! – Really will have to pull my horns in. I've started already, purchasing more locally-caught fish at only ten cents a pound. And I must say, the flying-fish have proved very tasty.

Another new reckoning has meant the giving of a personal dinner-party. Unfortunately *my* cooked rice proved very sticky, and fruit pie had almost rock-hard pastry.

I'm blaming the Baby Belling. Shame though, as was not consistent with my wine and candlelight embellishments.

★★★

About those flying-fish. Many locals fish at night, just off the reef, and this by means of a spot-light. Not so long ago flame-torches made of palm leaves were used – I expect this is still the case in less-sophisticated villages.

★★★

Elizabeth (WHO) was heard giving a lecture in the hospital classroom on child psychology. She explained how threats to children are a bad form of punishment.

"In my own country," she said, "mothers tell their children, if they aren't good, a policeman will get them. Do *you* have a similar expression?"

"Yes," someone responded, "*Our* mothers say, if *we* aren't good, Imatang (Europeans) will get us."

Amongst Gilbertese there is the custom of 'Bubuti'. To bubuti something means to desire it. Perhaps someone begs to have one's camera, for instance. This means one has to then give it away. It's usually asked for within a family group. That said however, Jenny's house girl, having viewed some of her photographic slides (presumably dealt with by sending film to Oz for development) felt *she* must bubuti them.

"I'll not part with them," said Jenny, this having caused much ill feeling. Guess one must hide away all things one definitely does not wish to give away.

***

We've had no rain for months, and the wet-season isn't due until about July. No-one seems particularly worried, but we Brits are now rationed with what is past saved rainwater. This may only be used for drinking and cooking, otherwise bore-water should be used for washing.

It is primarily us, we Imatang who create shortage, after all, *we* have ready use of house showers – even flush lavatories. To think though, when I was tiny and living in the Essex cottage, there was only an end-of-garden archaic, privy-lav.

Here however we encourage our nurses – and patients, to wash in the sea. If *we've* any real conscience, we should do so too.

Today – Sunday, I again attended the service at the Gilbertese church. It was given by a Gilbertese Reverend, the congregation seated cross-legged on the floor, all of us on woven straw mats.

Language-wise I didn't/couldn't, understand a word, but

enjoyed joining in the boisterous singing. Following a one-and-a-half-hour sit however, felt a bit stiff afterwards.

Should just say though, all Gilbertese looked very spruce: men in white shirts and white lavalavas, whilst many of the women and children had on white dresses. Little girls too, had as a plus, bows of ribbon in their hair – always beautiful hair, long straight and thick – whilst their brothers had theirs plastered down by water.

★★★

I've just attended a James Bond film at the cinema. The latter's a small, fenced-in compound, with a raised screen at one end. And here one takes one's own mat upon which to sit following a hand over of the twenty-five cent admission charge.

And the *following* Sunday, I joined another trip to Bikeman, the medical launch having been hired, this for one-dollar an hour.

We left at 8a.m., so arrived there early, a good long 'holiday' for those Gilbertese families also with us.

As often the case, on arrival at shallow water, we had to wade ashore to the beach. I myself however didn't realise. Didn't know that the Gilbertese regard a woman's exposed lower half as quite rude. They themselves have an opposite point of view, their exposed bosoms, that may flip-flop in the breeze, are not at all regarded as such.

Whilst women and children remained on the island, most men now went off fishing. Here though, those with guitars created music, it all now proving blissfully relaxing.

When the men returned with fish that I felt was a good catch, a fire was lit to cook those that were the smallest.

Some were of the parrotfish family, their jaw teeth fused into a parrot-like beak, used for scraping agar, as well as coral growth from reefs. They're so-named for the screech they give, heard when they get caught!

Gilbertise bite fish between the eyes to kill them. Some Imatang have tried to do this too, but are usually put off when they find they've bitten an eye-ball, meaning vitreous fluid bursts over their face. Err! I must say, revolting!

★★★

Have been to Tabiteuea with the Maternity and Child Health Team, this taking half an hour on the medical launch, plus on arrival some wading-water time.

The clinic was found to be held in a tiny thatched place, where just a floor of pandanus mats were spread out inside.

As far as children are concerned, the danger period is the weaning time when often the infant's weight remains static for months. Mothers may chew food before giving it to the baby; we are trying to encourage them to mash it with a fork, as well as to breast-feed for as long as possible.

There should then be no malnutrition, for the diet available can be quite adequate i.e.

Protein – fish, eggs
Fat – fish
Carbohydrate – breadfruit, babai, coconut & rice (imported)
Iron – fish, eggs
Minerals – fish
Vitamins – A & D sunlight, B fish & rice, C toddy,
particularly if not boiled or even heated for a short time.

Jan Crawford got some response to family-planning,;she was able to insert a vaginal loop. Her work is hampered by R.C. church missionaries though, who tell people this is something to be avoided.

Each mother who attended our session received a bar of soap, together with a bag of powdered milk (supplied by UNICEF), whilst antenatal women also received iron tablets.

As to us, we visitors, we received from the resident Gilbertese M.C.H. aid plus her mother, *moi moto* (coconut water) for drinks, then, before we left, a paw-paw each . I was also able to buy some breadfruit.

I was amazed to find a relatively new medical *jet,* small speedboat donated by the New Zealand Leper Trust, suddenly arrive to take us lot home. It merely got viewed however, as was seen to twirl around unstoppable upon the water. A bit like one of those Turkish dancers who manifests increasing frenzy, before developing a trance.

The boat that brought us was, however, there to be boarded, Jan and I soon wading out to climb upon it, even though it did mean pulling oneself upon its roof again, and avoid its suffocating interior.

Next day

A man admitted to the ward was found to be very sick. His illness had mainly to do with groaning whilst appearing both agitated and afraid. No other symptoms were apparent, he saying he felt as he did because of a 'spell' that had been cast upon him. A particular woman was responsible he said – his sister – following an argument he had had with her, about the rightful ownership of a certain stretch of land.

He'd friends who also practiced magic, one having said she would visit him each day and try to rid him of this bad influence.

When seen with this in mind, she'd firstly given him a massage, then wrapped a piece of white cloth around a leg, both attempts, I learnt, to drive away the evil.

★★★

It so happened today, that the woman with whom yesterday's patient, was said to have 'cast' a spell, also got admitted to the hospital. She somehow (? how) acquired a large wound across her back, nurses then informing me, we must witness a situation of, as it were, the best person winning, that's to say, according to the best magic.

"Don't be ridiculous!" I burst out.

★★★

These past few days I *was* pleased to observe, our male patient, recovering. Today however, he again became agitated, saying too that if his friend did not come to take him straightaway from the hospital (necessary), he would die.

No-one could reassure him. Sad to say this soon happened, all *attempts* to resuscitate – fruitless.

9th *May '68*
M.S. and wife invited all hospital staff to a formal dinner today. How we come to be in this colony leaves me thinking. It's how things were in India – years ago, for independence was gained in *1947*.

Can't say though I didn't enjoy today's event, although rather wickedly it had me (wrongly) feeling uppity.

We ladies all wore long dresses and white cotton gloves, gentlemen that strange tropical outfit known as 'Red-Sea Rig'. Do however feel that men themselves appear better when they have dressed-up, probably a pity they have so few opportunities.

10th May '68

Today, again by boat, although alone this time, I re-visited the dispensary at Betio.

I have come to the conclusion that I don't like Betio: it is especially hot, smells of oil, and looks like a shanty-town.

The usual chaos was seen within the dispensary; my return to the launch being one of exhaustion – mentally as well as physically.

Quite a swell was however experienced with its movement as I sat aboard the roof, feeling after a while I'd to hang on like grim death for fear of being rolled off. I could not though attempt to get down, for then would be bound to slip into the water.

It left me drenched and dizzy on arrival back at Tarawa, having nevertheless to face my afternoon's hospital work. Can't say today has been a day I can mark up as a good.

★★★

One of our Colony Nurses has decided she dislikes nursing, so had a talk with the C.M.O. to say she wished to return to her parents. These were dead, but she wanted to be with their spirits.

Although she was supposed to be on night-duty, I soon found myself informed of her failure to turn-up for her shift. Had said she felt unwell, it was therefore necessary for someone else to take her place.

Come morning though it was discovered. She'd got on a ship, which was now off to the Marshalls.

***

Have had a marvellous Saturday out sailing following teacher John's invite. Dave and Moira (also teachers) were asked as well, together with Rat-Man Joe.

John had the boat sent out from England, it having been made of fibre-glass. Anchored now in the lagoon, a small row boat with an outboard motor enabled all to soon climb aboard, it's mainsail thereupon received sufficient breeze, to get us over to Buota.

As common practice, we waded to its sandy beach, left what we'd carried, then had a blissful swim. Soon though, by now with an acquired appetite, it became time to light our fire, barbeque chops and sausages, and brew a pot of coffee.

Enjoying our eventual picnic, all of us chatted, learnt about each other's lives, as well our intentions on this island – why here, in this very remote place?

The moon was full on returning home, a good breeze lending excitement. I experienced added joy as taught now how to deal with both sail, as well as tiller.

***

Met again, Mr. Macoun – Chief of Colonial Police. He's here to tour these islands, and today came to the hospital.

I last met Mr. Macoun in the U.K. over at Farnham Castle – the time I received initiation for here. A charming man, he was interested to know how I'm doing.

"Settling down then?" he says, soft voiced and with warm eye contact.

Jenny and I, together with C.M.O. and wife, all found ourselves invited to his *official* welcome from Tarawa Police. That's how we arrived over in Betio in record time on H.H's launch, and this, unlike the medical launch is not at all smelly – in fact very comfy.

Here we were taken to the police grounds where I met many people I had not before seen, including King William – Mr. Kirby Jones, head of W.S. He's another charmer, though I should imagine, an unscrupulous businessman.

The police appeared marvellous in their uniforms – dark sulus with red cumberbands, they looking after us visitors in similar manner, drinks being served before the feast.

Mats had been set out on the playing field, a mat for each couple, whilst the feast was spread upon a large basket-type tray made of coconut fronds. And what a feast it was too – whole roasted chickens and crayfish, pandanus bread, and babai (rather like nutty porridge) onions and rice, with moi-moto to drink from the nut. I felt most honoured to share my feast with Mr. Macoun – for he was guest of honour.

Entertainment put on by Tabiteuean dancers followed, the police being now in grass-skirts, and bedecked with flowers. After a while we visitors were then hallowed, for they graciously wished us to join them. Being in the front row I was one of the first, but what could I do, other than

45

try 'the twist', which my Gilbertese partner possibly thought atrocious.

It soon however came to an end, Mr. Macoun receiving a presentation to which he replied with the aid of an interpreter. Or tried to – many dogs had decided it was time to have a fight, with the back of the audience involved, sufficient to create much screaming and hasty dispersal.

Although Mr. Macoun ceased to shout any more, the band started up, I myself now reminded of that gramophone record, the one in which Peter Sellers similarly battled, this with a speeding-up Irish band, until…

2nd June '67

Following Miss Blake's request, I took off with her to the M.C.H. Aides training school. Aides receive six months of training given by a Colony Nurse. They are village girls that have been recommended, and will deal with antenatal women and their eventual deliveries. Most villagers though prefer the old (untrained) village midwife.

We'd both, as usual, taken off on the medical launch, although getting atop its roof canvas involved me hauling Miss Blake up from beneath her armpits. She is rather frail, however managed to wade ashore at Terinibi.

On arrival on land the Colony Nurse with her aides was there to meet us before taking us to her house. Outside there was a bowl of water and a towel, enabling us to wash our feet before entering.

And here I might just point out, Gilbertese houses are of two styles. The first, on short stilts has a single room on the platform created, a thatched roof, and open sides. These have held up mats that can be unrolled to cover sides for privacy.

The other type – where now we entered, seemed more like a small house, this having several rooms. Divisions are created by fine strips of woven wood to make up walls, whilst all floor is covered with coconut matting and finer pandanus mats on top.

Having removed our flip-flops its entrance was found to be blissfully cool, whilst the Colony Nurse – so kind, soon supplied Enid Blake and myself with moi moto (from the topped coconut) to drink. Enid – of course, not wishing to have stained clothing, had brought with her a straw.

Later we moved to the schoolroom, here to fulfil our purpose – oral and practical aide examination. And must say, both of us were well pleased with results. These were bright girls.

Later still – I'm moved – for how well we Brits get looked after, Enid and myself found ourselves offered the customary meal. This had been prepared by the aides, we visitors eating alone so as to have first choice, what remained would then be eaten by the girls. And it was obvious there would be plenty, there being chicken as well as fish (this beheaded for our benefit) together with baked and boiled breadfruit, rice, and moi moto to again drink. Perhaps I should say I miss the salt, preparation though as always, very good. It's amazing what can be done using an open fire and earth oven.

After lunch, Enid, of course Sister Tutor, together with myself, did our inspection tour of the village. This was found to be spotlessly clean due to the zeal of the local policeman. He does his own tour each week and directs.

Residences all flank a wide road, whilst the bush beyond is especially attractive, because of a little real soil.

As we walked we saw old men smoking and talking in the maneaba, others beyond making fishing nets. Both copra and fish were spread to dry, although fish were covered in flies.

The launch journey back to Bikenibeu took longer than usual, as we had to stop and anchor in the lagoon in order to pick up a patient from another village. And here we had to wait sometime before those on shore saw us, then got organised enabling this to happen. The patient was then brought to board us by means of a canoe.

★★★

I recently delivered a pregnant woman, thought to have placenta praevia. I took the liberty of arranging for blood donors to wait outside ready to be called upon, for fear of a serious haemorrhage as she gave birth. Fortunately though, all was well, the placenta did not completely cover that baby's uterine exit as he entered this new world. Mummy's fine.

★★★

Rat man Joe's a good friend. He lives just a few houses away from me, and we sometimes share a meal together.

Joe, married, has a wife and two boys back home. He misses them terribly. Her arrival with him on this small low island, on hearing and seeing the bounding waves beyond the lagoon, she was so struck with fear she had to take that plane, or rather planes, straightaway back home again.

I'm well aware that re. Joe's friendship, I really must take care. It *must* remain platonic.

★★★

Jenny and I found ourselves invited to a wedding feast. The girl is the daughter of one of our hospital cooks. There was no church ceremony, but the bride was dressed in a wedding dress, whilst groom had on new white shorts and tee-shirt, as well as a decorating kowi.

What was however apparent, was the unhappiness of both. Perhaps in reality they did not care for each other, this marriage having been arranged by both sets of parents.

The bride, anyway, will have to endure her uncles' examination tonight. They wish to be satisfied she is (or was till now) a virgin.

Everyone sat on woven straw mats with a basket of food between two, all spread over the cinema compound. To me it felt as though we were a substitute film, for all squatting guests now found we received a constant viewing, this from a crowd that glared from beyond the wire-netting fence.

That aside, let me mention what we'd been given to eat: cooked pig with its liver, babai and rice. Coming from an enormous kettle all were served with drinks, this being very weakened tinned condensed milk.

After eating a band entertained us, the conductor wearing a tee-shirt inscribed with 'herd master'. Instruments consisted of several banjos, accompanied by a skiffle double-bass put together from a tea-chest.

Katerina sang her usual naughty songs, and when the

mats were all rolled we danced the twist. Actually not very easy on sand.

***

We've still had no rain of late on this island, so rationing of water continues. Some of the coconut trees have even been affected, and I am unable to plant my paw-paw seeds.

My luggage has arrived. Hurrah! And it has only taken two months – not three, to get here. Joe managed to chase after it for me, because it got delivered to the wrong people – the Catholic Church nuns.

***

I was visiting the TB ward when it happened. Poor, poor Maetese died in seconds. His cough produced a sudden haemorrhage; its gush, like a turned-on tap, so severe, and such as I've never seen before, meaning I could only be with him briefly before he choked to death.

***

Tabiteueans are always fighting. A particular session meant that Dr. Flood, our Gilbertese surgeon, had to leave us here, in order to carry out some called-for first aid there.

Several youths had had a quibble over the ownership of an eel trap, and as is common practice, toddy knives and spears became involved. One man was then killed, whilst another had his thumb chopped off. Several days however passed before our Doctor was called for, he then finding the wounds to be sutured had maggots. He also learnt that one man involved, after receiving a spear attack was left to die; this had gone right though him, in one side and out the other.

***

For the moment, we have only two cylinders of oxygen left in the hospital.

***

It's shocking to hear that most people employed by the Wholesale Society have been sacked, including even King William. This follows the loss of 36,000 Australian dollars. Some employees have said they failed to see that helping themselves was wrong. One man, clothing himself, actually thought it was right: a new pair of shorts – every day, with a new shirt for both a.m. and p.m.!

12th July '68
The beginning of my weekend really began Friday evening. Most of us Brits, by then off duty, then charged over to Bairiki to the Residency for cocktails, in order to celebrate the Queen's (plus my own) birthday.

On this occasion I found I bumped into quite a few new people. Already too it felt strange – indeed uncomfortable, wearing shoes again instead of flip-flops. All men no doubt felt likewise, since they were red faced and wriggling in their suits and ties.

Bruce McCaig met us at his doorway. Can't think how

he manages to remember everyone's name. Full glasses were then delivered to each one of us, before, as usual, we circulated and talked.

Time up, as on all these occasions, the National Anthem was played, its ending the signal to leave.

Those of us then back at our own village, dumped ourselves at that small hotel, this where men couldn't wait to fling off those jackets and ties, and also all the women those shoes. That past drinking orgy with nothing but tiny tit-bits had also left everyone feeling starved, happy therefore to heartily tuck into the pile of beef sandwiches that now circulated.

13th July '68

Continuing to celebrate the Queen's Bithday but with some formality, as it meant returning to Bairiki in order to witness H.H's inspection – not of troops (this place has none) but police, Boy Scouts and Girl Guides. Today he wore *his* uniform, this the hottest outfit imaginable, with, aside from the plumed hat, a large sword that had been slung around his waist.

The flag bearing the Royal Coat of Arms that was today supposed to be erected, unfortunately was not. Someone, last minute, had mislaid it. This meant the same Union Jack went up as well as down, myself only able to express another – "Oh dear…"

Formality was though soon over (fairly soon, for us lot, in that heat, had had to stand wearing hats and gloves), giving way to relaxation. This was when we trailed around a few stalls that had been set up bearing edible delicacies – albeit the ice-cream had melted, the jam tarts were very sticky, and orange juice very, very weak. These stalls though had been set up for the benefit of us Imatangs. Most locals were seen to be settled in an open maneaba, sprawled on mats to feed a babe, or else smoke an old clay pipe, another preparing their meal. The fish could be heard to sizzle and splutter, this in a fry-pan atop a small spirit stove.

Oh – there was too, amongst the stalls, a lucky-dip, and for just a few cents I dived in. My reward was a small strip of old cotton material. ?? A tie-belt –?? a head band. Dunno!

Throughout the afternoon the Gilbertese became lively again, we *ourselves* able to watch some play a game of volley-ball, and/or be involved in a boxing match, or else, within the lagoon, a canoe race. By this time though, I felt tired and had a headache – a touch of heat-stroke I think, so, having borrowed someone's mat, I flopped to take a nap in the shade of a pandanas.

Later, even though an evening feast had been prepared, I continued to feel just too tired to stay.

***

This past weekend I saw a 14ft dolphin half floating in the ocean, near to this land. As was obvious, it was unable to get back to deeper water. With courage a Gilbertese man leapt from his boat onto the dolphin's back, tied a rope around the animal, then managed to tow it ashore. Soon all locals, having killed the creature, carved for themselves great chunks of its flesh, carting it away by the bucketful, it with them regarded as a delicacy. Apart from this, a small boy was later seen, using its tail as a surf board.

Re. life here. A *potentially* dangerous situation is developing between Joe and myself, for there are occasions when I feel lonely. There is too – another potentiality, when work wise I've had to cope with lassitude. It's the climate here, so I don't, same as others, now charge about quite so speedily.

Enid has asked me to give the trainee girls some theatre lectures. Should it *really* be me?

***

Following Saturday
We'd a masked ball organised by Jenny and teacher Judith, in aid of the Girl Guides. All women also wore long dresses, and men their dinner-jackets, as well two pigs were roasted whole for the occasion.

Teacher Peter said he had just aquired a blow-up dinghy with a motor and would I like, within it, a zip around the lagoon? I said yes.

***

Have seen Peter a few times and we've been just *a couple*. Recently invited him back to my place for a coffee – not a good idea as he was now desirous of a certain development. He's had a letter from me to say I wish to have no further 'get togethers'.

***

The Tabiteueans of Tarawa gave a feast for Katikoa. This was to celebrate her hospital promotion to Staff Nurse. Katikoa received a New Zealand training in Fiji, this following on from the Colony Nurse training acquired here. Any further promotion means she'll also need to obtain a midwifery certificate.

★★★

A small boy appeared at my door with a bag of lobsters. Mmm… I thought, for a lobster with me is a favourite food. I did not know though (ignorant) its boiling takes place when it is still alive! Leastwise initially, so as I opened the bag to peer, pincer-like claws wishing to nip thrust forth. What a shame – I just couldn't buy.

And with reference to creature attacks, I recently adopted a ginger kitten. Sad to say though, now he is no more. Last night, awaking from a nightmare dream, I found on the floor this little creature was no more, for in a pool of blood its throat was seen ripped. This must have been the result of a *wild* cat's attack. Several of these prowl around outside, but also dogs – why I've now no shoes, only flip-flops.

On the positive side I have at last acquired a second-hand bike. This was not as it happens from our Kiwi, but Dr. Matthews. And certainly makes shopping a lot easier. Our doctor has returned to the U.K. to obtain a Public Health degree, and later, daresay, he'll be back to take over as Chief Medical Officer.

★★★

Life can though go on to appear horrible at times. This happened today. Jenny and I were partaking at work of a

55

mid-morning coffee, when just beyond the door, an open-backed truck – the driver in obvious panic mode – screeched to a halt. What we two now viewed was exposed to all eyes, it was a woman who had been found hanging, who must have been dead for sometime, for her livid and bloated face was seen to be swarming with ants. These were in and out of her mouth, up her nostrils etc. and etc.

It was learnt that the woman is the sister of one of our Gilbertese nurses, the gruesome event therefore aroused much curiosity. This was also the case with many young boys belonging to that family, they climbing to view her post-mortem taking place from the high window of our 'shed' mortuary.

***

Today a stabbing took place! This inside the prison and resulted in a bad injury. An emergency operation was required, but our theatre nurse could hardly push her way through the resultant crowd that had gathered. At first she was too afraid to try, that's until helped to do so.

***

Now this (with me) is a better topic. It has to do with Jenny teaching me to sail on her acquired Heron. It's rather like a largish surfboard (one gets wet) although it has a rudder to push down when in deep enough water, a helm for directional guidance, together with a rope for sail movement.

John Watson (teacher) was, I heard, nearly a goner on his. Out alone he got it spiked on the reef and it sank. Being some way from the shore where the current was very strong, how fortunate it was that a Gilbertese fisherman sighted his plight and got to rescue him.

Still thinking of boats, young Norman (V.S.O) went out Sunday on a Heron with his cook. Neither of them had a clue about sailing, but managed to drift quite happily across the lagoon. Trouble however began when they wished to return to land. They managed to reach shallow water where they could wade ashore, although this took them five hours, and with sharks taking an interest.

★★★

Several of us went fishing from the medical launch we anchored in the lagoon. All caught a large fish, including an eight pounder – 'cept me! It was Dave Edward who reeled in that big-un, this from the stern when we were on the move and returning home. He was proud as a kid and wanted to share it with the rest of us, but we insisted he took it home to show Moira.

★★★

Jenny, elected chairman of the tennis club, arranged a tournament. There's a court built by the Brits, that belongs to the hospital, and today I joined her to play a foursome match. Perhaps it's the heat, for my own athletic prowess didn't flourish, I did though enjoy the try. It began to get dark as the match finished, one witnessing, more or less as usual, a poppy-red sky.

I've indulged in even more exercise – dancing. And I must say this is thrilling. It's down at the hotel where in the evening one sometimes goes to meet others and indulge in a drink of lager. And anyone who ever happens to read this diary, can guess at my partner – Joe.

Well, it does him good too, and *he's* a very good dancer. He looks too rather boyish dancing, with his tall slim and lithe body, and wavy fair hair that becomes somehow more-so. Seems to be often a quick-quick-slow foxtrot (music by the way on a record-player), this with its special twirls around each corner.

It doesn't actually mean that any development has, or will, take place between the two of us, and anyway, Joe (and I) will shortly, be undertaking working visits to other tiny islands.

★★★

The House of Representatives today paid a visit to the hospital. I rather barged in on them after viewing the small group that late in the afternoon had gathered in the compound. Mistakenly thought it was the result of an accident, but no, and having made my presence known now had to be introduced all round, just at the point when they I daresay had been ready to start their tour.

However, finding myself forwarded I was conscious of the fact I was not, as it were, forearmed, so managed to nip ahead, snatch away the comics being read by some seated nurses, and get the cook to throw in the bin an empty corned beef tin.

One of these members, inspite of his tour, told me he was suffering from diarrhoea (though looked – and behaved OK). "I'd like some medication," he said, which meant I'd to now rush off to get some. Discovered though, was the fact we'd no more fresh little bottles, so with a sigh had to pour some perfectly good *other* stuff down the sink and use that one.

***

The arrival of a ship at last has left us with lots of exciting parcels to open. Several large ones are from UNICEF with equipment for the obstetric ward. That's good, for all metal trolleys are deteriorating with rust.

***

Saturday, and the student nurses, all so young and brown and Goya-esque, kindly invited me to a picnic. Ludicrously it was a party for a nurse who had recently got the sack. The PWD lorry also arrived more than half an hour late at the pick-up point, so that I felt hot and sweaty and already grumpy. Another hour was then spent touring to pick up various scattered relatives with all the food they'd prepared.

I think I must be getting past enjoying the antics of teenagers, as well the sort of food that's liked by them, lots of what gets called 777 sandwiches, the filling Japanese tinned fish. Even the cats won't eat this and I once found a fish hook in a patient's lunch.

We did indulge in a later swim although the nurses do not possess bathing costumes. They therefore swam in their lavalavas, it though quite acceptable for all to have bare bosoms.

***

The students of Atibuku put on another feast to include all Imatangs who attend Tangitabu church. The food was very good and eaten in a traditional manner from small woven basket-like pieces made from coconut fronds. (I know, I frequently detail the food eaten. Do I think I could starve? – No!)

Another tradition followed, with those in grass skirts clicking small sticks musically, whilst also singing and dancing. This always somehow seems lovingly enticing, something about them too leaves me feeling they're akin to mermaids.

As a responsive gesture the Gilbertese wished to hear an Imatang give a speech to thank them, something they delight in. They don't realise that most of us are rather averse to giving speeches, particularly on the spur of the moment.

***

Have finished giving theatre lectures to our student nurses. I thought they would all respond quite well to a test, if it wasn't made too difficult, and if a few clues were let out.

Sad to say, this was not the case. Certainly no one achieved a really top mark, the top girl only twelve out of twenty-five points, and I'm wondering if she really deserved that! Two girls acquired no points at all. I see now what Miss Blake has recently been feeling.

***

We have now at the hospital acquired a night-watchman. He is big and strong and strides around importantly with his big torch. One night he did get rather frightened, so went to fetch our Matron. It was learnt he had seen 'a body' through the window of the classroom, so Jenny went to investigate.

It turned out to be Jimmy (of course) the hanging, swinging, life-size plastic skeleton there to assist the nurses learning.

13ᵗʰ August '68

For a couple of weeks now, we have been hit by an influenza epidemic, this followed by gastroenteritis. At its height, the hospital received nigh on 300 outpatients in twenty-four hours, and having dished out thousands of aspirin tabs, we've greatly depleted our stock, especially as still awaiting last October's order.

Jenny was herself sick, so unable to work for just one day, I myself remained healthy, but felt almost at the end of my tether with half of our nurses away, and no orderlies.

On our worst day too, we had no water. P.W.D. failed to fill the tanks, they not being at work either; no cooked meals were therefore possible.

When the water did eventually appear (thank God) I had to get off-duty nurses to come and peg out all the laundry.

I can only feel sorry for all those who suffered for the virus was virulent and with many produced a temperature of up to 104°F. Many went on to develop pneumonia.

What then is remarkable, is the fact that an especially high death rate, did not occur.

★★★

When our Kiwi Elizabeth left us, because her time was up, I felt sorry waving her off as she boarded the plane. Another Public Health Educator from WHO will I'm told arrive, but I've not been able to learn exactly when. Also expected is a

Russian doctor from Kiev (can *this* be true?) but also, again, there's the query – when?

I have now moved into what was formerly Elizabeth's house and being nearer the hospital it will be more convenient. It is semi-detached (with Jenny my neighbour), has the usual attractive old-style thatched roof, and a lovely garden. Lovely for Tarawa, that is, with scarlet hibiscus and frangipani climbing its front wall, and a paw-paw and banana tree at the back. The nearby beach is too especially nice.

Also acquired (again) is a kitten. Actually two, one having six toes upon each paw. I wonder if this is a mutation due here and there to a raised level of radioactivity. This though is mainly further south, and where it's said to be the highest in the world due to the atom tests carried out.

The French are again carrying out tests, inspite of the many protests received from Polynesia.

When any ship in aid of us here on Tarawa goes to Christmas Island to pick up what it can, it'll load with as much as possible. This is often expensive equipment – even a couple of Land Rovers that just got left when the R.A.F. departed, not though a plane that has to remain to rot. There are even our jars of Nescafe, used for morning coffee.

★★★

Joe got me to give a First Aid lecture to the Boy Scouts. Am getting more used to this lecture business and can quite enjoy it. And Joe? Well silly man, I believe with me he is quite infatuated. I am trying to wean him without hurting his feelings. And anyway, it won't be so easy to 'pop-in' on me now that I've moved.

The school boys at K.G.V., when digging in the grounds, uncovered a pit full of numerous rounds of ammunition, this left after the war. Last week a Japanese tin helmet was also found at Betio, still with a skull inside it.

Next month – September, sees the twenty-fifth anniversary of the Battle of Tarawa. We expect some visitors.

16th August '68

Temone Flood, our Gilbertese surgeon – a cheery plump soul with strong legs like tree-trunks, today at morning coffee told the rest of us of an appendicectomy he performed (quite a while ago) out on Abemama.

With no mask or gloves he used a razor blade as a scalpel, and bent forks as retractors. Miraculously the wound healed and the patient made a good recovery.

His stories are often about the Japanese occupation and then liberation by the Americans. Again at Abemama, the locals became so pro-American, they wished the States to be their benefactors, as opposed to the United Kingdom. Temone though felt the opposite, and saw it his duty to guard the British flag.

1st September '68

Well yes – it's the month to celebrate the Battle of Tarawa, and today saw the arrival of a large white ship, the *Ninikoria*. A splendid sight, she glistened whilst cruising around our island beyond our turquoise lagoon, and beneath a clear blue sky. Everyone on shore dropped what they were doing to wave, as did too all of our many palm trees in the breeze.

★★★

A number of us colonials have formed a group to sing Gilbert and Sullivan; this with a once a week practice that proves much fun in teacher Fred's house. He had a piano sent out from the U.K. and it's sounding good, although I hope won't succumb to damp and deteriorate.

Out of the blue I have just received a letter from my father, this with psychological implications. He departed from my life when the war was on, so only became known when he arrived home in army uniform, and left a tin hat on my dressing table. That's when I was four.

His visit was though short-lived, for he soon returned to the army, never, till now, heard of again. Somehow he's found out where I am (here of all places!) and wishes to communicate. He's even signed himself, 'Your affectionate father'. But, am I *myself* desirous now of communication? – Well now…

★★★

There being remembrance of that war that was on here, has brought the arrival of an RAF plane, it stopping en-route from Honolulu to Singapore, where it was based.

I found myself invited to the airmen's reception at the Residency, and must say found it good to talk to some *new* people. I didn't get to bed until around 3am.

64

★★★

A nasty accident has occurred involving an ex-pat woman. She fell down the well in her garden – this about ten foot down, it was then sometime before she was rescued. How fortunate she was not badly injured, although it was an awful shock.

In addition to my two kittens, I have now acquired a mongrel puppy. Miss Blake says her lectures get disturbed by his shrieks when left, but I think (hope) this will soon settle down.

Our doctor Jan Crawford (my what a good looking woman with her dark curls, and athletic body), together with Kunu (getting *much* plumper) were terribly seasick when returning on the boat from their Family Planning campaign. So much so they'd to prematurely disembark at Beru.

It certainly was not their day however, for it then being necessary to get back aboard by being taken on a canoe, this capsized, and they had to swim for a while until rescued.

★★★

Our leper patients, having become very dissatisfied, sent a petion to Rouben, their chief elected member. They feel they should live in 'European style' houses, and as well receive pocket money of two dollars a month. They also wish to be given more rations, and stated that the jet-boat donated by the New Zealand Leper Trust is for their own personal use, as should also be the case regarding the UNICEF V.W.

The Ellice isles have supposedly made history with the first group of quads being born. Also – so locals say, the first murder! I'm sure people *have* been killed before, but it was not regarded as murder, for not till recently, was there any law.

The first Nurses and Midwife's Act has also in the Colony been passed, this meaning unauthorised people in the village. can not act as such. Perhaps though some will get away with it, for they do not usually go about the job for financial gain.

Some more girls have however 'passed-out' (and you know I don't mean fainted), receiving six months training here, from one of our Colony Nurses, before returning to Abaiang to otherwise live an ordinary village life, whilst receiving a nominal monthly payment.

***

Saleima, a few days ago, developed appendicitis. This required a surgical operation to remove this inflamed small sac attached to the lower end of the intestine, before it ruptured. So far as I know, this was not the case, the op therefore was carried out by our well-practised Gilbertese surgeon and his theatre nurse.

Saleima did not however recover, for she then developed tetanus – this with ghastly spasms, then died.

But why? – How? – I can't say, but I myself felt equally as distressed as the girl's many friends and relatives, with her during those last hours before she passed away, exhibiting an expression an uninhibited wailing.

Next day

Saleima's funeral was attended by myself, Matron Jenny, and the C.M.O. her body, taken from her uncle's place – one of our local doctors, when ready for burial. Prior to this, on *our* arrival, her coffin was put together. And will I ever forget, so much of a loud and clattered hammering was heard, as this was put together, use being made from a couple of our empty hospital boxes made of plywood.

At the same time Saleima's uncle edged over in order to speak to me, and turning to the ready made hole in the ground said, oh so seriously as he looked me in the eye,

"Dug it six foot down…" as though I might criticise, if it were not fully compliant.

3.

Today I was to have gone to Abaiang with the newly trained M.C.H. aides. Departure had on previous occasions been delayed, but this morning I really *did* think we'd get away. At Betio however, there we sat in the sun on wooden boxes, it was very soon blazing heat, for three hours. *Then* it was we learnt, *Tabaki* would sail tomorrow – at present its wireless was not working.

Next day

Arrived at Betio 8a.m. to spend a further two hours waiting. The ships wireless was still undergoing repair. But then. It happened!

The *Tabaki* is a landing craft on which all were packed like sardines. Once aboard, one had to take care not to be zonked, for the arm of the crane was loading petrol drums. At the same time some seamen were at the back constructing a lavatory, others undertaking (now!) some ship's painting.

At last though we were off. I found a spot on someone's mat atop some of the load-up, the following five-hour trip spent dozing.

On arrival at Abaiang which has a lot in common with all islands visited – small, near sea-level, and with many palm-trees waving, the girls and I were met by Colony Nurse Runga. Hatless, and shoeless, she nevertheless looked smart in her blue-white uniform with its shiny red belt. She helped me deposit my luggage at a local-style house having two rooms, before going on to take each aide to her respective village, by means of a hired truck. On the island there is too a doctor, Doctor Puta.

After a wash and brush-up, a bucket of water having been drawn for me, I visited the recently-constructed small hospital. This consists of two rows of small thatched houses, and a separate cookhouse where relatives of a patient can prepare a meal.

All post-natal mothers and babies were seen and found to be fine.

At the end of the day a prepared meal was brought me: chicken, babai, rice, and breadfruit washed down with tea. I missed the salt though.

The Island Executive Officer came to see me apologizing profusely about the loo. It's a pit-latrine with at present no seat, and when squatting one *does* have to stretch one's legs exceptionally far apart, taking care not to fall in the hole. He said though a box-seat *will* be provided. And as regards comfort, C.N. Runga has insisted I have *her* bed mattress.

Next day
After a fitful sleep, I was given a welcome breakfast of thick bread and butter sandwiches, with condensed milk tea to

drink. Then, by 8a.m. with C.N. Runga, we both took off on donated motorbikes, zooming along the sandy track to our first destination.

A meeting was held in the maneaba, villagers summoned by a head man blowing a conch shell. He then stated our business regarding function of the clinic huts. Actually, only three of the proposed eight have been erected, it was now pointed out that fines would be imposed if they failed to get on with the job.

Runga and I then went on to visit a further two villages, here where the role of those newly-rained aides was fully explained. A lunch in due course was offered.

On return to the hospital by evening I did a round with Dr. Puta. Most of the seventeen patients had post-flu symptoms, one person suffering severe protein/calorie malnutrition.

Next day

Discovered a 'cathedral'! (Though not much bigger than a large shed.) It has bells and a clock tower, but no pews inside.

I was back at the hospital early, here to examine nursing reports before breakfast. A man recently died of a compound leg fracture, also learnt, there were low stocks of aspirin and cough mixture. The dresser was urged to re-order, this before stocks were exhausted.

Breakfast was then *here* received: coconut bread together with *very*, very salt fish. It was marvellous though to have a cup of coffee, a luxury for the Gilbertese.

I've fallen in love with the peaceful atmosphere on Abaiang. Perhaps it's peace that won't last though, as many palm trees are being chopped down for islanders wishing to create a road for a bus. Several islets will then become linked. At present it can take all day to reach a sick patient, a canoe needed to go by sea.

Thursday
My return to Tarawa proved a most uncomfortable journey. It was also difficult to shelter oneself entirely from the sun, so I got very burnt.

Most of the deck where one settled was taken up with thatch, this also on its way to Tarawa. There were too pigs, chickens, and dogs.

Although my visit to Abaiang was brief – I would have liked to have stayed longer, I have gained some insight into the work of the M.C.H. team, whilst too observing some of its problems – those encountered on an outer island.

November, '68
High-ranking experts from time to time, arrive from the U.K. This is the case re. Miss Willmott, who has now been here six weeks.

Miss Willmott has given lectures concerning nutrition/malnutrition to our nurses, I myself am also able to attend. She has too, with Jan and Bob, carried out a nutrition survey on Maiana. Here the height, weight, and head circumference of all children was recorded, whilst questions asked about feeding.

A further survey was carried out on Betio, this where most of our malnutrition cases in the hospital come from. It's apparent from the survey that if the nutritional state of children *here* in particular, is to improve, markets of fresh fruit and vegetables – plus fish. must be established.

Most men on Betio *are* money earners without possession of land. He must too support numerous relatives. The W.S. should then I feel, import skimmed milk, this the cheapest form of protein in the world.

It is also evident that the local diet is deficient in vitamin B, so perhaps vitamin-enriched flour and rice could be imported.

The agricultural department, whilst continuing to undertake plant experiments, have obtained some success with: tomatoes, Chinese cabbage, and spinach. As well, not long ago a Fisheries expert visited the colony, he recommending establishment of the fishing industry, with excess sent to a likely good market in the U.S.

The outlook for the colony, is not at present very rosy, for the primary source of income is from phosphate mined on Ocean Island, which will be worked out by 1980. Copra is the only other export, but this can never be sufficient regarding support for the economy.

The Bishop has suggested everyone becoming resettled in other countries for these tiny islands will in time be able to support them.

How about supporting the family planning campaign!

***

Our matron Jenny has taken off for a tour of the southern Gilberts and is expected to be away ten days. I'm therefore to carry on with her work, which seems to be tied-up so much with directing rations and the food menu. As well I'll need to visit Bonriki to buy breadfruit, this being quite an amusing procedure.

★★★

The hospital has had a run of tragedies, leaving me rather depressed. Miss Blake, who herself has had a short tour, returned to Tarawa with a young European woman normally resident in a mission on Abemama also aboard. She was pregnant with a breech and near her time, it was unfortunate however that membranes ruptured, and she went into labour whilst still aboard.

She did arrive at the hospital without having given birth, although for a while had had a prolapsed cord. It meant the baby died.

★★★

Sadness aside the hotel has offered entertainment. Firstly using our own projector a film was seen; not a very good one, *but* one could see and hear it in comfort. Then (same place) a concert was put on by teachers John and Judith, these two playing guitars and folk singing ; this *was* good. A few evenings later, there was acting, a play put on by Bikenibeu amateur dramatics – *Arms and the Man*, by George Bernard Shaw.

★★★

This month it's the twenty-fifth anniversary of the Battle of Tarawa. An educational film has therefore been run, taken by the U.S. Marines, who during the last war, fought the Japanese who'd become resident on the island.

And what a bloody battle it was, with 1,000 Marines killed, whilst entirely wiping out (poor men) 4,000 Japanese. We expect veterans and tourists to arrive for 'celebrations'.

***

A battle of a very different type is at present underway regarding our swinging tennis tournament. And, believe it or not, we from the medical department are doing pretty well.

As well, on the tennis court, our nurses have had a party to commemorate the first birthday of the Trained Nurses Association. This was instituted by Jenny.

***

Did my bit for the Girl Guides Association. Went on a six mile hike with them, then cooked a meal off an open fire. Somehow this didn't seem quite right, not here in the tropics.

***

Have just attended a Hallowe'en Ball again to do with – well in aid of, the Girl Guides. It was marvellous to make it an occasion and wear again my long dress, zooming again over to Betio in what's now a new launch, a large and bright full moon seen just above the horizen.

Joe insisted on partnering me for he's still (why!) an ardent admirer. Honestly, I don't allow anything to develop, though there is an *element* of embarrassment when we two are part of a group, or *we two* have got invited to that dinner party. Trouble is, I do love to dance, so when he comes to collect me, I can't slam the door in his face. And anyway, his tour will soon be over.

***

Received is another communication from my father. And here's another difficulty. I know in the past, when a child, I longed to hear from him for I felt deserted. I'd then some picture in my head, imagining him to be like some glamorous (and loving) film star. These letters – and photos too, depict someone *entirely* different – basically stupid and *unlikable,* so…

With Jenny away, my current hospital role is proving a different, and sometimes difficult way of 'being'. It means working with people who've a different cultural background, often therefore a different way of thinking.

15ᵗʰ December '68
Many student nurses undertaking either their first or second year exam, have unfortunately failed. Guess we've to work harder with them. Those though, all eight who undertook their final exam; they have all been successful!

This evening a graduation party was held on the tennis court. Here it was found possible to decorate the netting with both coconut fronds and fairy lights, it then proving a good place for both feasting before dancing.

Unfortunately the hospital pig that we'd arranged to eat

here today, was found dead a couple of days ago. I saw it had no water so felt it suffered dehydration.

It had been left a few hours without its entrails having been removed, so I had some worry about contamination. I did however arrange for our hospital cook to chop and stew cook it, myself tasting, before it got served to patients and nurses.

It tasted OK, so *did* get served; and no-one's the worse for wear.

We have today too had sufficient celebration food: twenty-three cooked chickens, raw fish in coconut cream, breadfruit, te beki, cooked pumpkin and taro leaves, etc.

After the party, several hospital emergencies developed. One woman in labour but suffering a deep transverse arrest collapsed, although did revive after a rapid Caesar with one of our graduate nurses giving blood.

A Russian ship from Vladivostoc then stopped at our island because of an emergency, this a young woman with a ruptured fallopian tube due to an ectopic pregnancy. In this case some of her comrades could donate blood, these Russians, and ourselves, very interested in each other. I was surprised to see the women in both high-heeled shoes and mini-skirts, but they all looked very pale.

Next day
Last night proved hectic and I didn't get to bed until 5a.m. I managed though to get out to the airport in order to meet a new nurse who had previously been sent from here, to do a course in family planning.

She did not however arrive. It was rumoured that family-planning methods did not apply to herself, and although single, she was pregnant and unable to work.

Commemorations continue regarding the last war, a freighter having now arrived from New Zealand. Jenny and I – both of us, put up two of the engineers, then, this evening, we were all down at the hotel.

One blue joke followed another – on our behalf, but on the whole these visitors proved to be good company.

Next day (Saturday)
Many of us resident on this island, today went to Betio where speeches were given by both H.H., and a visiting American General who'd just arrived on a Hercules. He read a message from President Johnson, before a war-memorial was unveiled.

Rather ludicrously, just as the service began, a Japanese fishing boat was seen to arrive in Betio port.

Following the service a foundation stone was laid for the causeway that will link Betio to Bairiki. Some money for this will be American, although its eventual maintenance will be dealt with using British money.

Next day (Sunday)
Jenny and I were both up at the crack of dawn to see the Kiwis leave on their plane. An oil leak was though found to have developed from one of its engines, it therefore unable to take off.

A spare part was though cabled for, to be flown up from New Zealand. The huge Orion then arrived seven hours later, a new engine then dropped by parachute before it turned around without landing – off to Fiji to refuel.

It's now school holiday time. (So what a life teachers have! Eight long weeks not working.) I attended though a play they put on, and this did involve students: *The Long and the Short and Tall*. It was amusing to hear these students trying to adopt Welsh and Scottish accents.

Am myself attempting to get on with some gardening, this within the lepers' area, trying to get them to help. (Carefully of course, for their anaesthetic patches can easily be damaged.)

The lepers don't appear so discontent these days and I'm pleased with the progress we have all made. Some seeds I obtained from the Agricultural Dept.

The Red Cross is also working with them, some occupational therapy having been organised with some now working on embroidery, others making model boats. Some even make pandanus mats and baskets.

Their fishing is mostly at night with good catches enabling a lot to be sold to the hospital. This will earn them four to eight dollars.

3rd January '69

As may be seen from the date, our festive season has passed. Just before Christmas though, a friend of Jenny's arrived from Australia, adding I think to this time's enjoyment. She will be with us too for a couple of months.

A pig was cooked in the way Gilbertese cook it, within a pit dug several feet down into the ground, where a fire was then lit to create hot stones. The prepared *whole* pig, was then placed upon those stones and covered in sac, before the soil was put back atop.

Many hours were necessary for cooking to take place, but when it had, well – eating proved delectable. Jenny's friend was asked to undertake the first ceremonial stabbing for meat.

By the twenty-third, all hospital wards were seen to have been decorated beautifully, this by the nurses using crepe paper streamers, plus coconut fronds, and even coloured lights. A Christmas-tree was created using Casuria: it looks *almost* like the 'real thing' – decorated too in a similar manner.

The L.M.S. choir then sang carols in candlelit wards, this before distributing small presents to patients.

We Brits ourselves sang carols. This as we travelled in a truck around Bairiki, before going on to the midnight service at Tangitabu. Mince pies and coffee followed.

Celebrations continued, then ended New Year's Eve at, (naturally) our Scottish doctor's place. Here as midnight approached we all danced Scottish reels, then, as balloons descending from above, all sang 'Auld Lang Syne'.

An Oxygen cylinder was hammer banged at the church, the sound, indeed, much like that of a church bell.

★★★

My trip to Arorae has been postponed till the 15th. (Will I ever get there?) Meanwhile though I've continued to undertake preparations, Jan showing me how to insert Family Planning loops.

While in Betio I did too obtain my tinned food of corned beef for outer island habitation.

Getting back for return on the launch, a baby with gastroenteritis was then seen to have been brought aboard. Diarrhoea and vomiting has become prevalent, often initiating cases of malnutrition.

Joe is away on Ocean Island. Actually I'm rather glad.

23rd January '69
A week ago I was hustled to get myself with my heavy luggage aboard the *Temauri*, by 1p.m. Pharmacist Howard had failed to get anything ready for me until the last moment, which meant I myself had to assist him packing, the skimmed milk powder and boxes of soap, etc. On the good side, Jan lent me her kerosene iron, together with a pressure lamp.

The launch however remained stationary the rest of that day, night time too, I then, next morning, was informed we'd not be departing because the weather was very bad down south. A wild west wind would make it difficult to land on another reef island.

Well, how frustrating it then became, being daily directed to *ningabong and ningabong* – namely commute backwards and forwards to Betio from home for several days, until Friday that is, when my journey on *Temauri* was indefinitely cancelled.

I now booked myself to travel on *Nivanga* instead, this was said to take off the following Tuesday. Actually Tuesday changed to Thursday when, with difficulty because of a heavy sea swell, I did get myself with belongings aboard; it then – we were off!

I say *we*, for nurse Bontetake accompanied me. She however was told to remain on deck (how disgusting) whilst I was given a cabin. Poor Bontetake however became very seasick, I was then reprimanded by the ship's captain, for I told her to take a rest on my bunk.

★★★

Land was viewed at Nikunau where beacons had also been erected, marking where we were to enter the lagoon. Bontetake and myself went ashore here for a short period, being met by resident Doctor Eritane who lent us bicycles for a quick visit to the small hospital.

As the visit *was* short, I felt rather ashamed, presented as I was with both a shell neckless and small bag.

On board again the small deck was found to be covered with bags of copra.

27th January '69

After five days of travel Bontetake and myself were now ashore at Arorae, this where Bontetake will become resident, and I'll stay a few weeks.

A meeting was already arranged for us to meet members of the women's committee. These women have been acting as midwives during the absence, of anyone trained.

The hospital has been found to consist of – as is common, several local style houses, with too a cookhouse, small dispensary building, and place for the dresser.

Bontetake and myself will lodge in an island-style building, open at the sides but with mats to pull down for privacy. There is of course no furniture, but I've brought a camp bed with me, together with a mosquito net for covering.

My arrival has incited much curiosity from local young children who climb trees to stare down at me, or else follow my comings and goings.

Following occurs for instance when I'm off to the lavatory on the bicycle. It's a particular part of bare beach where faeces will soon presumably dry to kill off bacteria.

Meals are to be prepared for me and I've been asked if I like lobster. They'll be partaken of in the dresser's place.

As is usual practice one sits on a mat cross-legged on the floor, I am today finding an elderly, toothless old woman, made to sit next to me with a fan. She, so it seemed was designated to stop flies landing on my food, or even my face, for a tap-tap-tap was soon seen, or felt, whilst swish-swish swish with its breeze was constantly heard.

As I preferred to deal with such matters myself, I hope she did not think me rude when I asked her, basically, to 'stop it'.

***

And what can I say now I'm settled here and re. all meals I've gone on to receive? – Well, quite satisfactory –'cept I have been given octopus (*givers* regarding it as a delicacy) which *I* discovered tough as a piece of old leather. I endeavoured to chew my way through it though, so it didn't get left. Then, following this meal, I was presented with a hat and fan made from coconut leaves. Was it I wondered, a means of saying 'well done'? I should add, I have already made *my own* presentation to these people – stick tobacco, this requires tough chewing too, but not swallowing.

The island is small but highly populated having two villages: Tamaroa and Roreti. Each village has a fine small church and house for the Pastor, together with the usual type houses on stilts to catch more breeze.

There's no motor transport here as yet, but (like many Chinese) most get around on bicycles. There are though three motorcycles *medically* acquired and arousing envy. I'll get around on one!

★★★

I've spent six weeks on the island and this will be my report:

Arrived on Arorae 12.00 hours and here met by Dresser Tiota.

The hospital and dispensary I've found to be clean and tidy.

It had just three patients two of which, post confinement, were now receiving treatment for anaemia following P.P.H. Deliveries had been conducted at the hospital by local midwives, C.N. Bike now undertaking the role.

One of the hospital houses was found to be completely destroyed during the recent strong winds. The dresser is arranging for its reconstruction.

There are twenty-five patients on the TB register who regularly attend the dispensary to receive their treatment.

Medical supplies are adequate, some being stored in the kerosene refrigerater, this in working order.

Ninety-nine children up to the age of four years were seen from the village of Tamaroa, and forty-six from Roreti. The estimate is around half the actual number, although both villages are within walking distance of the dispensary where we were able to hold clinics.

The first triple antigen injection (against Diptheria, Tetanus, and Pertussis) was given to all children seen.

Further vaccine was then ordered by telegram for the second and third doses, which then arrived on R.C.S. *Tautunu*. A timetable staggering injections over several days, was then drawn up for C.N. Bike.

. All children were weighed, with height head and chest circumferances also undertaken and recorded for statistical purposes. Signs of vitamin deficiency, i.e. sore tongue, angular stomatitis, night blindness, was not apparent.

Impetigo and scabies was though very prevalent and treated at the dispensary.

Most children, until the age of about one year were breast fed, but from one to four years found to be underweight with, especially, thin arms and legs.

The mothers of two children with *severe* malnutrition were asked to admit them to the hospital, but as both refused, a compromise was suggested whereby mother and child attend the hospital alternate days. Skimmed milk powder was to be made into drinks at home, plus a dietary supplement rich in vitamins. A two hourly feeding regime of small amounts was to be undertaken. During my stay both children began gaining weight nicely.

A further twenty-eight children, less severely underweight, were issued with skimmed milk and vitamins.

Records were created and the importance of follow-up discussed with C.N. Bike.

Three talks on infant feeding, with particular emphasis on weaning were given in the maneaba.

School Hygeine Inspection:
227 children five to sixteen years were seen at the Island Council School and here most children were underweight.

For instance, in the nine to twelve years age group, fifteen were under three stone these children daily attending the dispensary for cod-liver-oil and vitamin tablets. Skimmed milk with them, can also be issued if thought necessary.

One child was noticed to have a painless skeletal deformity of the back. I referred him to Dr. Anterea as I thought he might be suffering from Pott's Disease.

A few cases of scabies and sores generally, were referred to the dispensary. thirty-four children with head lice could not be treated for no Lorexane was found in the dispensary.

Thirty-two children had severe dental caries.

More M.C.H. cards are required for two more schools having 190, and 110 pupils respectively.

AnteNatal:
Seven antenatal cases, all past twenty-four weeks' gestation, were seen – including Dr. Tiota's wife. One patient – Batera, thirty weeks gave her obstetric history: two breech deliveries, both babies dying soon after birth. This third pregnancy was also breech, but inspite of several attempts to persuade her to return with me to Tarawa for an eventual Caesarian section, she ardently refused.

Departed Arorae 0600hrs 5.2.69.

Ashore at Abemama for two hours 7.3.69, this where Dr. Simiona said he finds the recently supplied small boat *too* small, therefore a dangerous mode of transport. The hospital also requires a new primus stove.

Arrived at Betio 0700hrs 8.3.69

4.

Rather exhausted, so lacking in joie de vivre, Jenny said I could have a few holiday days to make up for recent weekends that were worked. Teachers Judith and John – *still* enjoying their lengthy free time suggested I join them – and not *just* for the day but three, we all sailing up north to initially stay with the pastor.

John, who's a small but perfect build, and whilst wearing just flowery boxer shorts, was seen to be as smoothly tanned as a native, arrived with his small boat for our pick-up. We three once aboard, then off to Buariki.

Here it's Tarawa's extreme north – the top, so having in due course waded ashore, we were met by the pastor. This well-sized man with kindly intelligent eyes, said he was ready with lunch. And well, the Gilbertese: how hospitable they always are.

The enormous pile of toddy bread *did* get consumed, washed down by lots of sweet tea, we visitors then making a reconnaissance of surroundings.

Looking across the ocean, here toward Abaiang, all ears were practically deafened by the noise of especially giant waves, foaming white as they broke on the reef, to sound like a rushing steam train.

The church has a little house set aside for visitors, it was here we all spent our first night, sleeping on mats.

Up early, the sky just rose pink, and lagoon grey green, all of us, with rucksacks again on our backs, were off for our trek by 7.30a.m.

Some coolness still, enhanced by the road, shady with lots of palm trees, from time to time we passed a few dwellings, locals here all calling their greeting – "Konamauri!" A rare island observance too was to see birds: terns, or curlews with wild sad calls that seemed related to their remoteness.

By 11a.m. we arrived at Taborio and the Catholic mission. Here, most daintily, four Sisters served us coffee in china cups, poured from a silver pot. Added was cherry cake. How pale *they* looked though, a sense of purpose however apparent with every gesture.

They were kind enough to then let us have a welcome shower, and before we left showed us around what appeared to be well equipped classrooms. I noticed however that the girls' lunch (eaten on Saturdays outside) consisted only of rice. We were glad to leave them our oranges, for them an absolute luxury.

Outside this village a short nap was taken until the sun was kinder. That sun was soon veiled, for a sudden heavy downpour occurred, we all then drenched to the skin. This was the first rain known to myself on Tarawa, although it turned out to be short-lived.

We'd soon though been able to shelter in a maneaba, this where a policeman greeted us. He'd supplied us with moi moto to drink, although I believe he must have already partaken of something stronger, judging by his rough and ready mode of being. He then insisted we have more refreshment this time in his house.

Here a light-skinned young woman shook hands, the

policeman informing us her father, on the island during the war, was English, both of them obviously proud of the fact. She now continued to receive from him (now back home) a handsome allowance.

Back in the maneaba we partook once again of an afternoon nap, until, with the sun less burning, we were off again on our trek.

Our first north passage was soon arrived at, and although the tide was falling, water was still above our knees. We would be wading out to two boys with a canoe, but before we took off, the last house offered us another moi moto. This was paid for by means of tobacco sticks, with chewing gum for the children.

The strong young males wielded their paddles through what was here, with the now lowering sun, gold speckled water, until we were over the deepest part of this passage.

Up here, the islets arrived at are of course. still part of Tarawa. They still present tall feminine palms, whilst small beaches have fine clean sand that looks almost like caster sugar. What we also saw, to the left, before the wall of coral, our milky calm lagoon, whilst to our right equally near, that ocean, for here it had turned around. Now – just before dark, up above we saw herons, they like small planes circling above, this before coming to land.

Soon though we could now clamber off the boat, for another splash through waist-deep water. To me it seemed like we'd arrived at the end of the earth. We'd covered, I was told, o'er both land and sea today, nigh on eighteen miles.

Our arrival was then at Pastor Nabena's place. What a marvellous feeling it was too to rest, after our strenuous day followed by the cleansing wash in the bath-house. As is commonly created this was a small hut on stilts housing a large tub of water, its splashes draining away through its floor gaps.

Well then there was hot sweet tea to drink, and with the smell of fish cooking, a supper to look forward to.

Not late to bed, sleep was unfortunately marred by the mossies. We'd been supplied with nets but they'd too many holes in them to be at all effective.

Off again early morning, our back packs were now much lighter, all gift 'payments' having by now been given away. We'd turned around to 'get back', and our journey less exploratory was now much shorter, so completed in just one day.

Today, with the lagoon tide 'out' we must cut across much sand to Buota, the motorboat up there, being left for the time being. This was a hot trek, six miles totally without shade, but in due course from the air-field – *by bus!*

Jenny supplied a beer, after which I went to bed.

P.S. I cannot at all remember this adventure. It's there though, written in the tatty old diary from which now, many years later I type.

Queen's Birthday. Occurring for me on this island – once again!
The Information Office sent the hospital ninety paper copies of flags to be used as decoration. They represent St. George, St. Patrick, and the Union Jack but need (? occupational therapy) to be coloured.

Our few private patients – Brits, and all men – refused to take the matter seriously, for when I went to see how they were doing, found myself practically attacked by paper darts. The night-nurses and chronic TB patients did their bit though, using coloured pencils to fill in. Yes, their copies *did* end up colourful, except roses got filled in green, shamrocks red, whilst the background of the Union Jack was vivid mauve.

★★★

Recently, a male mental patient, sitting if not *with* the pigs, near them whilst remaining silent and gazing out to sea, could not be persuaded to return to where he would receive care. I'd talked and talked for some time with him, but my efforts failed, so I went in search of the two dressers in the leprosarium to help.

Returning to where I had left the patient, we three now found he had waded out to sea. He probably planned to take his own life as by now nearing the surf of the reef.

Both dressers had soon however plunged into the water, and just in time managed to rescue him. Afterwards they told me a large shark had neared them, though they lived to tell the tale. Lepers with their canoe arrived, but as the tide soon receded all had had to wait in the heat, until again it rose.

★★★

Hospital staff recently had a little stimulation when the amateur dramatic society put on another play – Gogal's *The Government Inspector*. I must say, it proved a first-class effort, very much enjoyed by all, and very funny in places. Especially when Bob Martyn's moustache blew off into his soup. The play might almost be a description of Tarawa at present with all departments here sprucing themselves for the impending visit of the High Commissioner.

***

Both first, and twenty-first birthday, calls for Gilbertese celebration, years between not considered significant. Nora though, employee in the hospital, was able to organise a feast for her baby son.

During my time on Tarawa all feasts have been seen to get more and more Europeanised. This time then, there was an iced birthday cake with 'Happy Birthday' iced atop, plus one small candle to be lit. 'Happy Birthday' also got sung – in English .

***

Once again, having delivered theatre lectures to the second-year students, I set them an exam, wishing to see how much had been absorbed. Answers in general were then funny, vis. Trendelenburg position is to make the patient's intestines fall out. Catgut is fed to babies with malnutrition. They were also disappointing.

***

Last weekend Bob took Jenny and me out in – or is it on, his Gilbertese outrigger canoe. Although Gordon was also invited, he became impeded at the hotel. Eventually though he managed in *his* boat to cross the lagoon at great speed, then join us in that 'other world' for the barbecue.

These B.B.Qs have become common practice, much enjoyed, and today, return journey, I played my part, up and down the actual outrigger, with it skimming very fast across the water.

Very stiff following.

★★★

My turn to give a dinner party.

I think Jenny was rather shocked that I should have mundane sausages on my menu, especially as I'd given her likewise for lunch. (Maid Momoa had bought too many for me.)

The meal then proved an awful failure for once cooked, taking them from the oven I dropped the tray. My guests though, wishing to be kind, insisted they got scraped up from the floor, then dabbed clean before serving.

The cork then broke in the Reisling – I'm not used to dealing with wine, drinks then needing to be served using my tea strainer.

★★★

Jenny is due to go on leave soon. Before this happens with myself taking over her role, a visit for me to see Ocean Island has been arranged.

9ᵗʰ May '69
Temauri left Betio at 8a.m. she was soon bobbing around like (another) cork on the rough water.

93

I was the only passenger not getting sea sick, all the others frequently staggering off to vomit overboard, whilst I tucked into my meal. And what glances they gave me as if to say, "How could you!"

Eventually Ocean Island was seen, this a *real* island, rising high above what remained a churning sea. It looked though brown and scarred, for much machinery is used to obtain earth phosphate. The choking dust this creates already blew in our direction,

Tom Ainswoth the District Commissioner met me once we'd landed, pleased to meet a visitor; for he did, I learnt, find it difficult, and back-biting, dealing with B.P.C.

Islanders, employees, however receive much generosity, good salaries, and houses built for them with free electricity. Luxurious food, cigarettes, and liquor is also available, whilst a swimming pool and library has been built. And yet, as Tom said, their traditional culture has disappeared, and they are less happy. There are no singing toddy cutters, no one wears flowers, no traditional feasts, and sailing is prohibited as it's too dangerous. Neither do planes land here, it really is cut-off.

For Tom it's the last place on earth to have been sent to govern. And in this respect he finds little to do, much time therefore spent reading a novel. Stress was noticeable, for a tremor, quite a tell-tale shaky hand was observed as he poured himself an early glass of wine. Poor chap!

The hospital was found to be extremely well equipped with trained staff consisting entirely of Australian Nursing Sisters. Much food is supplied from tins, thrown into the sea, if shown to have the least dent. Fresh frozen food also arrives from Australia (cheese, eggs, meat, plus fresh fruit and veg.) not at the moment though, as there are dock strikes.

Next day – Friday

I exaggerated my story somewhat re. food that's shipped (or not shipped) to Tarawa, so before I left to get back there, Dr. Brownridge supplied me with a box of paw-paws and limes, together with bread especially made for me, and a Christmas pudding.

Two Ocean Island policemen then boarded with me, to get off at Nonouti. They'd learnt political disturbance brewed there.

18th May '69

All Brits on tenterhooks today – the wedding of Peter and Rosie.

This was at the Roman Catholic Cathedral which I'd not before visited. And how impressed I was. It has been built entirely by local craftsmen, with, inside, beautiful stained glass windows imported from France.

Rosie was half an hour late, all who awaited her were therefore anxious albeit a string band played attempting to calm us. But – when she *did* arrive, weren't we stunned! – stunned by her exquisite appearance.

How incredible it *then* was, for following the ceremony the choir burst forth to sing the 'Hallelujah Chorus'.

All attenders returned home, there to change clothing for evening dress, before taking off to the hotel. Initially we all obtained a sit-down feast. And well – how 250 people were *here* accommodated its hard to say, other than it *was* managed, boys serving us efficiently, whilst also looking marvellous wearing their red waistcoats, and long dark sulus.

Aside from the crayfish and pig etc. we'd many bottles of wine to drink, all soon set up, happy and energetic to dance. It went with a swing until 1a.m.

Gordon awoke me at lord knows what time, shouting through the bedroom window, asking me to "open up". He wanted another party – not on! as far as I was concerned, definitely not.

★★★

His Excellency, the High Commissioner Sir Michael Gass, will be spending a week or so here. Today he examined all of the hospital, accompanied by our doctor and C.M.O., they were (phew!) obliged to be dressed formally, wearing their jackets.

26th May '69
Aboard *R.C.S. Ninikoria* and arriving Abemama 9a.m.

27th May '69
Dr. Simiona has made arrangements for myself and C.N. Teretia to be accommodated in C.N. Aole's house. A *new* nurse's house using permanent materials is though almost finished, construction organised by the Island Council.

Wednesday 28th May '69

The hospital here consists of eight 'houses' – one recently blown down in strong wind, a cookhouse and dispensary. Dr. Simiona is urging construction of bath houses, also the repair of two nakataris.

One person suffering from leprosy is not isolated.

Treatment sheets should be created and a TB register kept.

Adequate stocks are available.

Simiona prepared a main meal for me – a proper sit down meal at a table, he having managed to 'bubuti' both steak and cabbage from *Ninikoria*. He too sat at the table although did not eat, instead drank beer, soon then became very chatty, (?? a bit of a rogue).

Thursday 29th May '69

8-9.30a.m. Assisted in giving treatments to outpatients.

10-2.30p.m. Now at the clinic at Tabiang ten miles away, using the motorbike as transport. This does though need a new kick-starter, Katerina and myself at present needing to run 100yds to get it started.

The children seen here are healthier than those seen previously on Arorae. Weights on the whole are satisfactory, with avitiminosis not encountered.

Twenty-four were given the first Triple Antigen.

Two antenatal cases were examined.

A talk was given re.(1) Infant feeding, and (2) Family planning, this latter not however appreciated, it being a Roman Catholic village.

Katerina's mother living here, prepared our lunch – moi-moto to drink, then superb breadfruit and fish. "Why my husband married me" she let out.

I had hoped to then see the school children, but this did not prove possible for their day finished at 1p.m. Instead Aolete took me to see the newly completed airfield.

Evenings are rather lonely. Teretia has deserted me for her family, so I'm on my own. Two young V.S.O.s were kind enough to give me a lump of pumpkin that they've grown themselves, this island able to be fertile.

Friday 30th May '69
8-9.30a.m. Observed treatment in the hospital, before taking off on the motorbike again. This was to the child clinic at Katirake seven miles away, accompanied by M.C.H. aide Tamateara.

The clinic hut was observed to be in good condition, as well as clean and tidy. Its aide, Aolele, had not had to deal with a delivery for one month, she therefore joined us visitors who were to see all children in the maneaba. She obtained hand-washing water for us, together with a primus stove to sterilise our syringes, these for vacinations.

In due course a medical card was filled in for each child, all receiving a general examination prior to their 'prick'. In general all were found healthier than those I saw on Arorae, with better teeth and skin, and cleaner heads. Neither was avitiminosis apparent, except with a few children seen to have muddy sclera (? vitamin A deficiency).

The attendance at a morning and afternoon session was of thirty-six children – eight new cases.

A short talk was also given on infant feeding, and family planning. One person is already on Volidan, three new cases obtained.

A few early antenatal women were also seen with their Hb checked, and urine tested. (Urine was collected in a coconut shell.) Ferrous Sulph. and multivitamins were also handed out and people told to collect skimmed milk.

One was not then allowed to feel tired, but welcome, for Teretia's relatives had arranged for raucous singing in grass-skirts to be heard.

31ˢᵗ May '69 (Saturday)
Outpatients seen at the hospital, a.m. only, then p.m., have been able to write in my accomodation.

Here, seating myself in the doorway of its raised platform, I've been able to dangle my legs. Inside too, I *do* have a small table constructed from boxes, albeit it's rather wobbly.

This house is of Teboa wood with Pandanus thatch, and inside the floor is covered with mats. Beyond, I have my own well, I *now* have mastered the art of drawing water with the pole, also my own little bath hut – unfortunately shared with a huge old toad, and my own privy. (So I don't have to use a nakatari out to sea, running the narrow plank to get there, and where inside I felt I should have a parachute, as I was afraid of being blown out to sea.) It's very quiet, apart from the company of a mangy old cat who steals my dinner if I don't watch it, and a few dogs and chickens which wander in and out of the place.

The only local transport here is a decrepit government truck, it is therefore great to instead have the motorbikes –

albeit, I've probably mentioned, one must run along with for around a hundred yards to get it started.

I'm not likely to see much of local doctor Simiona, he being busy on his home visits. Yesterday, a man sailed from Aranuka, thirty-four miles away, to get him to return with him and treat a child, suffering it would seem from meningitis. Simiona was unable to return with him though, but sent the man back with the medication of S-Dimidine and Tetracycline. Here's hoping the child still lived on his return. It's a pity Nabatiku didn't divert *Santa Teresa*, to get him then take him to Tarawa.

P.M. Found myself given in the maneaba, an official welcome by the president of the Island Council. He still calls himself King of Abemama, and is in fact a descendant of the old king. His speech was however in English, to which I had to reply. It was fortunate also that my reply could be in English, just a few sentences at a time which he translated.

I then handed out my presentation of tobacco sticks* before enjoying the usual fantastic feast, this followed by everyone becoming involved in dancing the Scottish reel. It had only recently been taught by a former visitor and was obviously loved, the same dance tonight having many repetitions.

Before leaving I heard another speech, myself of course needing to respond.

* *At this time disease was not yet associated with tobacco.*

1st June '69 (Sunday)
Attending the hospital outpatients.

2nd June '69

Initially saw again the hospital outpatients here, before taking off to Baretoa six miles away. Another child clinic was held assisted by aide Toti, although no special hut has as yet been built for the purpose. Thirty-two children were never-the-less seen, followed by my usual talk re. infant feeding and family planning.

3rd June '69

Had to be up at 3a.m. to catch my boat on the incoming tide. This was on the one carrying copra, the UNICEF boat found to be too small.

The journey to the tiny islet of Abatiku took around two hours. It's not been visited since last December, I am therefore required to take supplies for aide Tenonga.

On arrival I learnt that Tenonga has been unable to undertake birth deliveries, for the village untrained midwife remains predominantly popular. Tenonga is now pregnant herself, *so...*

Twenty-five children were here seen at a further clinic for *their* vaccinations. No gross malnutrition was encountered, although impetigo and scabies was predominant, and a few sore tongues seen, together with angular stomatitis. (? Pandanas)

A hygiene inspection was later undertaken at the school. All children here were found to be reasonably healthy, apart from the discovery of some head lice and dental caries. (Same in U.K.)

There was not time for a full village inspection, this though undertaken by the police constable who'd come up with us, an effort being made to enforce the by-laws. What I *did* see was nakataris in good condition, the beach around being uncontaminated. Water-wells were also fenced, whilst cooking and eating utensils were kept on platforms beside each hut. Good thing too for many dogs and fowls wandered about.

Returned to my place 6p.m.

4th June '69

4th June '69

Another day spent attending the hospital outpatients, and then hygiene inspection at Moarine school. Aside from observing dental caries, one child was found to be deaf and referred to the doctor.

This evening attended a fine dance at Baretoa, performed by old men. More speeches followed.

5th June '69

Following my hospital attendance I had a clinic today in Tebontibike. Again there's no clinic building, so feel the aide here should try to be active.

Attempted my own word on the matter, as this evening I'd *another* requested clinic, this given at the Government station where eleven children were seen.

6th June '69

The clinic today was held at Tebanga where there is no aide to assist, and no hut. There were though only nine people seen.

A feast and dancing was then arranged on my behalf, and staged in the maneaba.

7ᵗʰ June '69 (Saturday)
My last working day here. And p.m.: as expected – a wonderful send-off.

5.

Up at 5a.m. to get the truck up to Tanimainiku. Aolele's belongings were now many, and included a hastily salted pig, and live chickens. Coming aboard with us too was a leper for review.

Our ship was not though seen to arrive, but I heard via the radio she'd be late, around 11.30a.m.

On this occasion the rough trip back to Tarawa was because of a dicky fuel pump.

★★★

Of late I've mostly been working with our dear matron here – Jenny. It's preparation for *myself* taking over her role, this when she will undertake her long deserved leave after running this establishment – or, perhaps I should say – establish*ments*. Will I be up to the task?

Sad to say a few days ago she was in the V.W. van, returning from the fresh fruit run from Bonriki (herself not driving) when it crashed into a coconut tree. Jenny was not badly injured – thank god, (neither the driver) but had a bump on the head, and was shocked, has had to spend a couple of days as a patient in her own hospital.

Her packing as a consequence is much behind, for

now too there's the spate of parties that always precede a departure.

★★★

Jenny was off today, Joe and I and others observing her incoming plane, before she undertook what's always thought, with those remaining, a sad departure.

★★★

Miss Blake will also soon be leaving, and due to Miss Schofield's British Report (for Parliament) we will not have another British Sister Tutor delegated. Instead two Gilbertese girls, soon arriving back from their overseas courses will undertake this work. Rather thrown into it I fear.

Having now to undertake my *new* hospital role, I've many outside commitments I must pass on to someone else, including that to do with Girl Guides with its newsletter and treasury. A home-made cake sale is organised, I am hoping to raise some funds. My own cake today though has raised a misunderstanding. My maid felt I made it for her so it disappeared.

★★★

Today I went over to Betio with Miss Bently (our new WHO), this to organise our future Maternity and Child Health programme.

Betio – how strange today it seemed. Sadly it remains the worst spot on this island, and the most populated, 5,000 living in just a quarter of a square mile. It's where most of our malnourished infants come from. There are too only two trained aides, with as yet no clinic huts. I hope Miss B. can help sort out the chaos.

★★★

I've a new plan for this term in office: improving the trainee nurses' diet, the pig-man to bring pumpkin tips twice a week with the cooks shown how to deal with them, a nurse's club night on Mondays, this alternating with film nights, and a course of lectures for hospital orderlies.

★★★

Yesterday was my birthday – oh dear – twenty-nine years . I've now marked up two thirds of my stay here. After my Sunday morning tour of the hospital, teacher (and friend) Judith came for coffee which extended into lunch whilst playing records, and then we took off for a lively sail on her 'sailfish'. We'd more tea and record playing on return, for she has lent me Britten and Mahler.

Come evening Judith went home, but Joe arrived to take me out to dinner. In due course a whole bottle of wine was drained between us. Both of us couldn't stop talking…

Diary to be continued…

Also by Mo Rudling

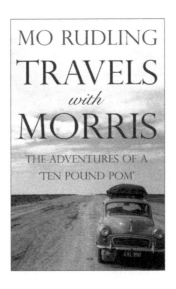

During the early 1960s, Mo Rudling and her friend Julie travelled thousands of miles around wild Australia with their faithful companion Morris, a sky-blue second hand Morris Minor. They spent many nights in the bush, sleeping in a two-man tent and cooking over just a camp fire and tackling unmarked roads (self-taught Mo having passed her driving test only a few weeks prior to the trip).

Inspired by the diaries she kept during her travels, this book will appeal to any fans of travel writing, particularly those who are attracted to the land of Oz as well as those who, like Mo, decided to emigrate there after the Second World War.

Read on for an extract from *Travels with Morris…*

CHAPTER 1

Getting Away

I had arranged to meet Julie at Melbourne airport as she was flying over from Tasmania. (And no, Tasmania is not what you might think, not a mental state!) So, with all equipment loaded both inside and atop Morris, I straightaway took off. The prospect of a year or more of wandering and an anticipated trail of thousands and thousands of miles, not only enticed, but having relinquished all serious commitments infused my mind with a wonderful sense of freedom.

At the airport I experienced no difficulty recognising my former ship-board acquaintance, she a somewhat frail looking and slightly stooped individual, although like myself she was still in her early twenties. In addition to the large rucksack that was mounted upon her back, she carried a smallish black box. This might well have contained say – a canteen of cutlery (inappropriate) or even a selection of surgical instruments (possibly useful). Yet neither was the case, instead as soon I learnt, a dissembled clarinet. Julie under no circumstances intended to abandon her daily practice.

My comments about Melbourne will be brief, it's a bustling metropolis with trams running down its thoroughfares. Well at that time Julie and I did not wish to prolong our stay as we were more intent on getting to Alice Springs as soon as possible. Melbourne's latter syllable incidentally is pronounced 'bun' not 'born', it's a sure giveaway that you are a Pommy, or Pom if you don't. This strange nickname has stuck as the English migrants were once thought to resemble pomegranates – and well, maybe they still do!

That aside Australians generalise and say Sidney for pleasure, Adelaide for culture and Melbourne for business. What sort of business? I had wondered, although contemplating its buildings and people I failed to form an opinion. Many buildings are Victorian, well set back from those wide streets, where, so it seemed, no lady (that's to say besides Julie and myself) ever dared set out bereft of hat and gloves.

Although in summer the temperature can soar above a hundred, we found it cool although sunny and bright. Our need there was to purely stock up on last minute provisions. Last minute I say – in fact this took all of two days necessitating accommodation at the YWCA.

When eventually on our way we stopped in the suburbs to buy fresh meat. Although locating a butcher had proved somewhat difficult, it does not in retrospect seem credible, that with our intention of crossing practically uncharted deserts, we managed on such a mini expedition to lose the car. Neither of us had taken into account where we had left her when we took off to shop.

There followed three hours of frantic enquiries together with a report lodged at the local police station. But then, on our way to another sub-station, on our second bus journey suddenly we spotted her, our own little vehicle patiently awaiting our return.

'Stop! Stop!' we both shrieked like mad women, one of us at least at the same time pressing the bell so hard...